CREPE COOKERY

by MABLE HOFFMAN

CREPE COOKERY

Author: Mable Hoffman
Co-Author: Gar Hoffman
Research Assistant: Jan Robertson
Publisher: Bill Fisher
Editor: Carl Shipman
Editorial Consultant: Grace Williams
Book Design: Josh Young
Book Assembly: Nancy Fisher
Typography: Marcia Redding
Photography: George de Gennaro Studios

Paperback,
    ISBN: 0-912656-50-6
Hardcover,
    ISBN: 0-912656-51-4

Library of Congress Catalog
    Card No. 76-3230

H. P. Book No. 50, Paperback
H. P. Book No. 51, Hardcover

© 1976 Printed in U.S.A. 4-76

H. P. Books, P. O. Box 5367
Tucson, AZ 85703
602/888-2150

WHAT'S A CREPE?

Crepes are not new, even though more and more people are enjoying them these days. This culinary delight is almost as old as civilization itself, and through the years has been perfected in humble kitchens of the world. In spite of its common beginnings, the crepe has become synonymous with elegant dining and gracious living.

Crepe is a French word meaning a very thin pancake. It is used in referring to the final filled culinary creation and also the "pancake" made from batter. Though the French word has been adopted in the United States, the crepe is by no means exclusively French. Almost every nationality developed its own version: The Hungarian *palacsinta,* Mexican *enchilada,* Chinese egg roll, Jewish *blintz,* Italian *cannelloni,* Russian *blini,* Scandinavian *plättar,* Greek *krep* and others.

There are two ways to pronounce the word—equally acceptable in North America. You can rhyme *steps* with crepes, or rhyme it with *grapes.* Whatever you call it, by any pronunciation, everybody agrees they're delicious.

Crepes are fun, simple, elegant, economical, versatile and delicious. This book will help you explore and enjoy them. There are recipes for main-dish crepes with the gourmet touch—using spices and flavors that compel appreciation, but do it with gentle persuasion.

There are desserts—Oh yes, there are desserts! The dessert crepe may be cookery's most delicious concoction. This book has more dessert recipes than any other kind—they are so good I found it hard to stop!

There are also recipes for simple basic crepes which please because they seem more fundamental. In this category it's easy to improvise and invent—using whatever you have—just as the first crepe cooks did. Leftovers change dramatically when they take an encore wrapped in a crepe, perked by whatever kind of sauce or adornment you choose.

I have given you a lot of batter recipes with suggestions on how to use them. These batters work well with the new upside-down crepe griddles, as well as traditional pans and skillets.

There are some international favorites here, besides the French-inspired dishes. Some of the foreign recipes are my own—I serve them to family and friends. I borrowed the flavor and mood of a popular foreign food but translated it into an easily-prepared and different crepe.

Crepes invite experimentation—you'll do it too! The sauce recipes help you in doing just that. The possibilities are endless. So have fun with *Crepe Cookery.* Enjoy the food and the compliments that are sure to come your way.

HOW TO DO IT UPSIDE DOWN

Dip preheated upside-down crepe griddle into batter in 9-inch pie pan. Hold crepe griddle in batter for only a moment. Gently lift griddle up and turn over. If cooking surface gets too hot, crepe batter will partially adhere to surface, then fall back into dipping dish. Either lower the temperature on your range, or unplug the appliance for a couple of minutes before continuing to make crepes.

Immediately return griddle to heat. Cook until batter loses its wet look and—with most batters—a very slight browning begins to show on the edge of crepe. The first crepe is often lacy and unattractive. Plan to discard the first crepe.

Remove from heat. Turn griddle over; gently loosen outer edge of crepe with thin plastic, wooden, or Teflon ®-coated pancake turner or spatula. Crepe should fall onto stack in plate. If not, loosen center of crepe with the spatula.

HOW TO DO IT RIGHT SIDE UP

It is not necessary to grease pans having a non-stick coating. Others should be brushed with oil or butter. Heat pan over medium-high heat. With one hand, pour in 2 to 3 tablespoons of batter. At the same time, lift pan above heating unit with your other hand.

Immediately tilt pan in all directions, swirling the batter so it covers the bottom of the pan in a very thin layer. Work quickly before batter cooks too much to swirl. Return to heating unit and cook over medium-high heat.

Cook crepe until bottom is browned. Then carefully turn with spatula. Use a Teflon®-coated or plastic spatula for coated pans. Brown other side for a few seconds. Remove from pan with spatula; stack on plate or tray.

SHAPE YOUR CREPE

Crepes take a variety of interesting shapes, depending on the kind of filling or the way you want to serve them. Try several shapes to determine which ones appeal to you. Many of our recipes suggest the popular fold-over, but you may prefer another shape for variety or eye appeal.

Which side of the crepe do you want to show on the outside? One side of a crepe is always better looking than the other. Those made in traditional pans are usually more attractive on the side that was cooked first. The other side is lighter and rather spotty. Those made in the upside-down griddles are brown on one side (the side against the griddle). Look at both sides before you add the filling so you end up with the crepe showing its most attractive browner face.

FOLD-OVER—The most popular crepe shape. Versatile for entrée or dessert recipes because it is easy to shape and shows off the filling.

HALF-FOLD—A handy fold for Crepewiches and Eggs Benedict or any other recipe when filling is too large for other shapes.

Place crepe, best-looking side down, on board, plate, or in pan. Spoon or spread filling along center of crepe.

Place crepe, best-looking side down, on board or plate. Place filling on half of the lighter side of the crepe.

Fold one side over, covering most of the filling.

Fold crepe in half.

Fold over opposite side, overlapping first fold.

ROLL-UP—This is a good shape for most fillings that can be spread over crepes. Appetizers in this form are easy to cut into bite-size pieces.

BURRITO ROLL—The traditional shape for a burrito is also handy for fillings that are likely to become runny when heated. Folded sides help keep the mixture inside the crepe.

Place crepe, best-looking side down, on board or plate. Spread filling over other side, leaving about 1/4-inch border around edge.

Place crepe, best-looking brown side down, on board or plate. Spread filling over light side leaving about 1/2-inch border around edge, or spoon filling into center of crepe. Fold right and left sides over filling.

Starting at one side, roll up like a jelly roll.

Starting at the bottom of the crepe, roll up. Make sure the folded sides are included in roll.

Continue rolling until entire crepe is in a roll or log shape.

BLINTZ or POCKET FOLD—Keeps filling inside crepe—especially for any recipe to be sautéed or deep-fried. When deep-frying, place the filling on the brown side of the crepe.

Place crepe, best-looking side down, on board or plate. Spoon filling on center of crepe.

Fold right side over slightly more than half the filling. Then fold left side of crepe over filling, slightly overlapping right side.

Fold bottom of crepe over almost half of filling.

Fold top of crepe down over both sides, almost to center. A popular variation of this fold is: Fold both sides over filling; then fold bottom and top.

CUPS—A real surprise shape, yet so easy to do! Use crepes as liners in muffin pans. Then there's no limit on what you can choose for fillings. Be sure to select crepes free from holes or cracks so egg-and-cheese mixtures won't leak out.

Carefully place small crepes, best-looking side up, into greased muffin pans. Gently tuck one into each space, carefully arranging the ruffled tops into an interesting pattern. Fill and bake according to the recipe.

CREPE SUZETTE FOLD—Excellent for creamy or butter-filled recipes. Shape crepes in hot liquids (melted butter, fruit juice, or liqueur) with wooden spoons, forks, spatulas, or turners.

Place crepe, best-looking side down, on board or plate. Spoon filling on center of crepe. Fold in half.

Fold in half again, forming a triangle four layers thick.

WEDGE—One of the easiest ways to shape a crepe—commonly used for appetizers because it is bite-size. And you'll want to cut crepes into wedges for dipping—either dessert fondues or appetizers.

Place crepe on board or plate with correct side up, depending on recipe. Spread filling, leaving about 1/4-inch border around edge. With a sharp knife, cut wedges.

STACK or GATEAU—Impressive dessert, appetizer, or main dish. Crepes are stacked with filling between each layer. Crown top with cheese, whipped cream, or other sauce.

Place crepes, best side up, on board or plate. Spread filling over each crepe, leaving about 1/4-inch border around edge.

Stack one filled crepe on another, to desired height. Usually it is easier to spread each one before stacking, but if filling is runny or hard to handle, you can spread each crepe after it is added to the stack.

THE BATTERY

Afraid to try a crepe batter? It's merely a combination of eggs, flour, milk and butter or oil. Think about the simplicity of a crepe batter and you'll realize it is easier to make than a cake, pie, biscuit, yeast bread or many other foods you normally prepare without a second thought. Many people are afraid of crepes because they haven't tried them. Although crepes have a foreign name and international reputation, they can be as homey and All-American as you want them to be.

There are so many good all-purpose batters it may be difficult to decide which one to try first. Notice that some of them have very little butter or oil—while others are *much* richer. Also, batters contain varying numbers of eggs. Naturally, you will choose the one that looks best to you. All will work well with the new crepe griddles as well as the traditional pans, unless I've indicated otherwise. You may want to try on of the packaged crepe mixes or frozen batter available in your supermarket.

You have a choice of several ways to make a crepe batter. Mix it, blend it, beat it with a whisk or even a wooden spoon. I suggest you use the method that is most comfortable for you.

After you have combined the ingredients, it is a good idea to let the mixture stand for an hour or more before cooking. Leave it at room temperature for an hour, it is not absolutely necessary to make it ahead of time. However, letting it stand allows the flour to expand and some of the bubbles to collapse. If you find the batter is slightly thick, thin it with a tablespoon or so of milk or water. Thinner batters produce more crepes, and they are extra-thin—if you are using an upside-down griddle.

Batter is usually smooth after you let it stand. Don't be concerned if there are tiny lumps—just strain the batter through a sieve. Incidentally, thinner batters seem to work best with traditional crepe pans.

Many all-purpose batters are *basic* batters. They may be used for crepes to contain meats, vegetables, appetizers or even desserts. However, I have given you a variety so you can match batters with individual foods or for specific purposes. For example, the dessert crepes have some sugar, fruit juice or liqueur so they will blend expecially well with ice creams and fruit or cream fillings used in dessert crepes.

Then there are the specialized batters. The *Lo-Cal Batter* is for calorie-counters, and the *Egg-Substitute Crepe Batter* is compatible with a low-cholesterol diet.The Wheat Germ and Yogurt flavors should appeal to those interested in nutritional values. Remember, each batter has an individual look and taste. Some will be slightly thicker, others will brown faster, each has its own texture.

Packaged crepe mixes and frozen batter produce very good crepes. They save time and alleviate any fear you might have about preparing a batter from "scratch." The mixes contain the proper blends of dry ingredients and the frozen batter is pan-ready when thawed. Both types store well and are ready for use on a moment's notice.

Have fun trying the batters and matching them with your favorite fillings.

All-Purpose Crepe Batter I

Our favorite! Ideal for upside-down crepe griddles as well as traditional pans.

4 eggs
1/4 teaspoon salt
2 cups flour

2 1/4 cups milk
1/4 cup melted butter

Mixer or whisk method:
In medium mixing bowl, combine eggs and salt. Gradually add flour alternately with milk, beating with an electric mixer or whisk until smooth. Beat in melted butter.

Blender method:
Combine ingredients in blender jar; blend for about 1 minute. Scrape down sides with rubber spatula and blend for another 15 seconds or until smooth.

Both methods:
Refrigerate batter at least 1 hour. Cook on upside-down crepe griddle or in traditional pan. Makes about 32 to 36 crepes.

All-Purpose Crepe Batter II

Good basic batter made with butter or oil.

3 eggs
1/4 teaspoon salt
2 cups flour

2 cups milk
1/4 cup melted butter or cooking oil

Mixer or whisk method:
In medium mixing bowl, combine eggs and salt. Gradually add flour alternately with milk, beating with electric mixer or whisk until smooth. Beat in melted butter or oil.

Blender method:
Combine ingredients in blender jar; blend for about 1 minute. Scrape down sides with rubber spatula and blend for another 15 seconds or until smooth.

Both methods:
Refrigerate batter at least 1 hour. Cook on upside-down crepe griddle or in traditional pan. This is one of the thicker batters. You may want to add 1 or 2 tablespoons of milk or water for thinner crepes in traditional pan. Makes about 30 to 35 crepes.

All-Purpose Crepe Batter III

Rich batter made with lots of butter.

4 eggs
1/4 teaspoon salt
2 cups flour

2 cups milk
1/2 cup melted butter

Mixer or whisk method:
In medium mixing bowl, combine eggs and salt. Gradually add flour alternately with milk, beating with electric mixer or whisk until smooth. Beat in melted butter.

Blender method:
Combine ingredients in blender jar; blend for about 1 minute. Scrape down sides with rubber spatula and blend for another 15 seconds or until smooth.

Both methods:
Refrigerate batter at least 1 hour. Cook on upside-down crepe griddle or in traditional pan. This is one of the thicker batters. You may want to add 1 or 2 tablespoons of milk or water for thinner crepes in traditional pan. Makes about 30 to 35 crepes.

All-Purpose Crepe Batter IV

Basic batter made with evaporated milk.

3 eggs
1/8 teaspoon salt
1 1/2 cups flour

1 small can evaporated milk (2/3 cup undiluted)
1 cup water
2 tablespoons melted butter

Mixer or whisk method:
In medium mixing bowl, combine eggs and salt. Gradually add flour alternately with undiluted milk and water, beating with electric mixer or whisk until smooth. Beat in melted butter.

Blender method:
Combine ingredients in blender jar; blend for about 1 minute. Scrape down sides with rubber spatula and blend for another 15 seconds or until smooth.

Both methods:
Refrigerate batter at least 1 hour. Cook on upside-down crepe griddle or in traditional pan. Makes about 28 to 32 crepes.

Egg-Substitute Crepe Batter

Designed especially for low-cholesterol diets.

1/2 cup cholesterol-free egg substitute
2 cups flour

2-1/4 cups skim or non-fat milk
2 tablespoons cooking oil

In medium bowl or blender jar, mix or blend until smooth. Let stand about 1 hour. Stir and cook on upside-down crepe griddle or in traditional pan. Makes 26 to 32 crepes.

Note:
This batter has a greater tendency to stick than most batters. If sticking occurs, apply a thin coating of cooking oil to pan or griddle before cooking each crepe, or as required.

Rich Crepe Batter

Deep yellow color and delightfully rich egg flavor.

4 egg yolks
4 whole eggs
1 1/4 cups flour

1 cup milk
1 tablespoon cooking oil

Mixer or whisk method:
In medium mixing bowl, combine whole eggs and egg yolks. Gradually add flour alternately with milk, beating with electric mixer or whisk until smooth. Beat in oil.

Blender method:
Combine ingredients in blender jar; blend for about 1 minute. Scrape down sides with rubber spatula and blend for another 15 seconds or until smooth.

Both methods:
Refrigerate batter at least 1 hour. Cook on upside-down crepe griddle or in traditional pan. Makes about 25 to 30 crepes.

Instant Flour Crepe Batter

Basic batter made with instant flour. Makes crepes immediately without a standing period.

3 eggs
1/4 teaspoon salt
1 cup instant flour

2/3 cup milk
2/3 cup water
1 tablespoon cooking oil

Mixer or whisk method:
In medium mixing bowl, combine eggs and salt. Gradually add flour alternately with milk and water, beating with electric mixer or whisk until smooth. Beat in oil.

Blender method:
Combine ingredients in blender jar; blend for about 1 minute. Scrape down sides with rubber spatula and blend for another 15 seconds or until smooth.

Both methods:
Cook on upside-down crepe griddle or in traditional pan. This batter does not have to be refrigerated before using. You can use it right away. Be sure to stir batter occasionally as flour has a tendency to sink. Makes about 16 to 20 crepes.

Lo-Cal Crepe Batter

A good batter for calorie counters.

3 eggs
1 cup flour
1/4 cup instant nonfat dry milk

1 cup water
1/8 teaspoon salt

Mixer or whisk method:
In medium mixing bowl, combine ingredients. Beat with electric mixer or whisk until smooth.

Blender method:
Combine ingredients in blender jar; blend on low for about 1 minute. Scrape down sides with rubber spatula and blend for another 15 seconds or until smooth.

Both methods:
Refrigerate 1 hour or more. If batter separates, stir gently before cooking. Cook on upside-down crepe griddle or in traditional pan. Makes 18 to 22 crepes.

Basic Dessert Crepe Batter

Good basic dessert crepe.

4 eggs
1 cup flour
2 tablespoons sugar

1 cup milk
1/4 cup water
1 tablespoon melted butter

Mixer or whisk method:

In medium mixing bowl, beat eggs. Gradually add flour and sugar alternately with milk and water, beating with electric mixer or whisk until smooth. Beat in melted butter.

Blender method:

Combine ingredients in blender jar; blend for about 1 minute. Scrape down sides with rubber spatula and blend for another 15 seconds or until smooth.

Both methods:

Refrigerate batter at least 1 hour. Cook on upside-down crepe griddle or in traditional pan. Makes about 20 to 25 crepes.

Orange Dessert Crepe Batter

Add an orange touch to your dessert.

3 whole eggs
2 egg yolks
1/4 teaspoon salt
1 cup flour
1 tablespoon sugar

1/2 cup orange juice
1/2 cup milk
2 tablespoons cooking oil
1 teaspoon grated orange peel

Mixer or whisk method:

In medium mixing bowl, combine eggs and egg yolks with salt. Gradually add flour and sugar alternately with orange juice and milk, beating with electric mixer or whisk until smooth. Beat in oil and orange peel.

Blender method:

Combine ingredients in blender jar; blend for about 1 minute. Scrape down sides with rubber spatula and blend for another 15 seconds or until smooth.

Both methods:

Refrigerate batter about 1 hour. Stir before using. Cook on upside-down crepe griddle or in traditional pan. Makes about 20 to 24 crepes.

Chocolate Dessert Crepe Batter

Special crepe batter for chocolate enthusiasts.

3 eggs
1 cup flour
2 tablespoons sugar

2 tablespoons cocoa
1 1/4 cups buttermilk*
2 tablespoons melted butter

Mixer or whisk method:
In medium mixing bowl, beat eggs. Add flour, sugar, and cocoa alternately with buttermilk, beating with electric mixer or whisk until smooth. Beat in melted butter.

Blender method:
Combine ingredients in blender jar; blend for about 1 minute. Scrape down sides with rubber spatula and blend for another 15 seconds or until smooth.

Both methods:
Refrigerate batter about 1 hour. Cook on upside-down crepe griddle or in traditional pan. Makes about 18 to 22 crepes.

*If you don't have buttermilk, add 1 tablespoon lemon juice to 1 1/4 cups regular milk.

Vanilla Dessert Crepe Batter

Vanilla adds a special touch to dessert crepes.

3 eggs
1/2 teaspoon salt
1 1/2 cups flour
2 cups milk

1 tablespoon sugar
2 teaspoons vanilla extract
2 tablespoons melted butter

Mixer or whisk method:
In medium mixing bowl, combine eggs and salt. Gradually beat in flour alternately with milk. Then add sugar and vanilla extract. Beat with electric mixer or whisk until smooth. Beat in melted butter.

Blender method:
Combine eggs, flour, milk, salt, sugar, and vanilla extract; blend on low for about 1 minute. Scrape down sides with rubber spatula and blend for another 15 seconds while adding melted butter.

Both methods:
Refrigerate about 1 hour. Stir batter before cooking. Cook on upside-down crepe griddle or in traditional pan. Makes 32 to 35 crepes.

Brandy Dessert Crepe Batter

A good dessert crepe without butter or oil.

3 eggs
1 cup flour
1 cup water

1 tablespoon brandy
1/2 teaspoon salt
1 teaspoon sugar

Mixer or whisk method:
In medium mixing bowl, beat eggs. Add flour alternately with water; then brandy, salt, and sugar. Beat with electric mixer or whisk until smooth.

Blender method:
Combine ingredients in blender jar; blend for about 1 minute. Scrape down sides with rubber spatula and blend for another 15 seconds or until smooth.

Both methods:
Refrigerate batter for about 1 hour. Batter has tendency to separate while refrigerated, so stir with spoon or spatula before cooking. Cook on upside-down crepe griddle or in traditional pan. Makes 18 to 22 crepes.

Rum Dessert Crepe Batter

Thinner than most, this batter works well in either traditional pans or upside-down griddles.

3 eggs
3/4 cup flour
3/4 cup milk
1/4 cup water

2 tablespoons sugar
2 tablespoons rum
2 tablespoons melted butter

Mixer or whisk method:
In medium mixing bowl, beat eggs. Gradually add flour alternately with milk and water; then sugar. Beat with electric mixer or whisk until smooth. Add rum and melted butter; beat until blended.

Blender method:
Combine ingredients in blender jar; blend for about 1 minute. Scrape down sides with rubber spatula and blend for another 15 seconds or until smooth.

Both methods:
Refrigerate batter about 1 hour. Cook on upside-down crepe griddle or in traditional pan. Makes 18 to 22 crepes.

Lemon Dessert Crepe Batter

Light crepes—perfect with fruit or cream fillings.

1/4 cup butter
1/2 cup cold water
1/4 cup milk
2 whole eggs
2 egg yolks

3/4 cup flour
1 tablespoon sugar
1 teaspoon grated lemon peel
1/4 teaspoon salt

To clarify butter: Melt 1/4 cup in small, heavy saucepan. Skim off and discard the surface foam. Spoon the clear butter on top into a measuring cup; discard milky solids at the bottom of the pan. Makes about 2 tablespoons of clarified butter.

In medium bowl or blender jar, combine clarified butter with water, milk, whole eggs, egg yolks, flour, sugar, lemon peel, and salt. Mix or blend until smooth. Makes 15 to 20 crepes.

Graham Cracker Crepe Batter

Unique flavor and texture for dessert crepes.

4 eggs
1 cup flour
1 cup finely crushed graham crackers
    (about 12 to 14 crackers)

2 cups milk
1/4 cup melted butter

In medium mixing bowl, beat eggs. Gradually add flour and crushed graham crackers alternately with milk, beating with electric mixer or whisk until smooth. Beat in melted butter.

Refrigerate batter at least 1 hour. Stir batter before cooking. Cook on upside-down crepe griddle or in traditional pan. Keep heat at medium (or slightly lower than heat for All-Purpose Crepes). Makes about 25 to 30 crepes.

Wheat Germ Crepe Batter

Wheat germ contributes texture and a distinctive flavor.

2 eggs
3/4 cup flour
1/4 teaspoon salt

1/3 cup wheat germ
1 1/4 cups milk

Mixer or whisk method:
In medium mixing bowl, combine ingredients and beat with electric mixer or whisk until smooth.

Blender method:
Combine ingredients in blender jar; blend for about 1 minute. Scrape down sides with rubber spatula and blend for another 15 seconds or until smooth.

Both methods:
Refrigerate at least 1 hour. Stir batter before cooking. Cook on upside-down crepe griddle or in traditional pan. Makes 18 to 22 crepes.

Potato Crepe Batter

Lend a German flavor to your filling.

3 eggs
3/4 cup milk
1/2 cup mashed potatoes
1/2 teaspoon salt

1/8 teaspoon pepper
1/8 teaspoon nutmeg
6 tablespoons flour
3 tablespoons melted butter

Mixer or whisk method:
In medium bowl, beat eggs; then add milk and beat on low speed until blended. Add potatoes, salt, pepper, and nutmeg. Add flour gradually while beating on low speed; beat until smooth. Pour in melted butter and beat until mixed.

Blender method:
Combine ingredients (except butter) in blender jar; blend about 30 seconds. Scrape down sides of jar with rubber spatula and blend another 10 seconds or until smooth. Add butter and blend until butter is mixed.

Both methods:
Let stand at least 1 hour. Cook on upside-down crepe griddle or in traditional pan. Stir batter occasionally when cooking.

Bran Crepe Batter

Bran makes it truly different.

3/4 cup flour
1/4 teaspoon salt
1 tablespoon sugar
1/3 cup All-Bran® cereal

2 eggs
1 1/4 cups milk
2 tablespoons melted butter

In medium mixing bowl, combine flour, salt, sugar, cereal, and eggs. Gradually add milk, beating with electric mixer or whisk until smooth. Add butter and beat until blended. Refrigerate at least 1 hour. Stir batter and cook on upside-down crepe griddle or in traditional pan. Makes about 18 to 22 crepes.

Yogurt Crepe Batter

Special for yogurt fans!

1 cup flour
1 tablespoon sugar
1/4 teaspoon salt

4 eggs
1 cup plain yogurt
1/4 cup water

In medium mixing bowl, combine flour with sugar and salt. Make well in center; drop in eggs, yogurt, and water. Beat until smooth. May be cooked right away or refrigerated several hours.

Batter is rather thick, so you may want to add another tablespoon of water for cooking in a traditional pan. Makes 18 to 20 crepes.

Pancake Mix Crepe Batter

If you like the convenience of pancake mix, try these crepes.

3 eggs
1 1/2 cups milk

3 tablespoons cooking oil
1 1/2 cups pancake mix

In mixing bowl, combine ingredients. Beat with whisk, spoon, or rotary beater until smooth. Cook on upside-down crepe griddle or in traditional pan.

These crepes have more bubbles than most batters.

Beer Crepe Batter

Really good with meat and seafood fillings.

2 eggs
2 egg yolks
1 teaspoon salt
1 cup flour

1 cup beer
1 tablespoon sour cream
1 tablespoon melted butter

Mixer or whisk method:
In medium mixing bowl, beat eggs and egg yolks with salt. Gradually add flour alternately with beer. Beat with electric mixer or whisk until smooth. Stir in sour cream and butter.

Blender method:
Combine ingredients in blender jar; blend for about 1 minute. Scrape down sides with rubber spatula and blend for another 15 seconds or until smooth.

Both methods:
Refrigerate batter about 1 hour. Cook on upside-down crepe griddle or in traditional pan. Makes 18 to 22 crepes.

Herb Crepe Batter

You'll enjoy the aroma while cooking these!

3 eggs
2 cups flour
1 cup milk
1 cup chicken bouillon

1/4 cup melted butter or cooking oil
1/2 teaspoon dried tarragon leaves, crushed
1 tablespoon finely minced parsley
1 tablespoon finely minced chives

Mixer or whisk method:
In medium bowl, beat eggs. Gradually add flour alternately with milk and bouillon. Beat with electric mixer or whisk until smooth. Beat in melted butter or oil. Stir in tarragon, parsley, and chives.

Blender method:
Combine all ingredients except herbs in blender jar; blend for about 1 minute. Scrape down sides with rubber spatula and blend another 15 seconds or until smooth. Stir in tarragon, parsley, and chives.

Both methods:
Let stand for at least 1 hour. Cook on upside-down crepe griddle or in traditional pan. Stir batter several times during cooking. Makes about 25 to 30 crepes.

Blintz Crepe Batter

Easy to handle and light! Makes an ideal batter for blintzes or other crepes that are browned after they're filled.

2 eggs
1 cup flour

1/2 teaspoon salt
1 cup water

Mixer or whisk method:
In medium mixing bowl, beat eggs with electric mixer or whisk. Gradually add flour and salt alternately with water. Beat until smooth.

Blender method:
Combine ingredients in blender jar; blend for about 1 minute. Scrape down sides with rubber spatula and blend for another 15 seconds or until smooth.

Both methods:
Refrigerate batter about 1 hour. Stir before cooking. Makes 14 to 18 crepes.

Chinese Egg Roll Batter

When freshly cooked, these are very easy to fold. They are ideal for crepes to be used like egg rolls.

1 egg
1 cup lukewarm water
1/4 cup cornstarch
1 1/8 cups flour

1/2 teaspoon salt
1/2 teaspoon almond extract
1/2 teaspoon sugar

Mixer or whisk method:
In mixing bowl, beat egg with electric mixer or whisk. Add water, cornstarch, flour, salt, almond extract, and sugar; beat until smooth.

Blender method:
Combine ingredients in blender jar; blend for about 1 minute. Scrape down sides with rubber spatula and blend for another 15 seconds or until smooth.

Both methods:
Refrigerate batter for 1 hour, if possible. Cook on upside-down crepe griddle or in traditional pan. Makes 12 to 14 crepes.

While being cooked, this batter does not brown as readily as other batter recipes. When filled and fried, it turns a nice golden color.

Crepe Mixes & Frozen Batter

These products are all supplied with mixing and/or use instructions on the container. Mixes are located near the pancake mixes in your supermarket. Frozen batter can usually be found in the frozen-food area.

Aunt Jemima Dinner & Dessert Crepe Batter by Quaker Oats Co., Chicago, IL.
Available as a frozen batter in two 8-ounce cartons, and as a box containing 14 ounces of dry mix to which you add eggs and water. The frozen batter is ready for use once it has thawed. Both of these products provide a flavorful, slightly sweet crepe which is thick and rich appearing. They are especially good for dessert crepes.

Krusteaze Crepe Mix by Continental Mills, Seattle, WN.
This dry mix is supplied in a 14-ounce carton. You add water and eggs. Crepes made from this mix are good-tasting and have a very pleasant smell while cooking. Available only in the western states, primarily in the Pacific Northwest.

Creative Crepes by McCormick-Schilling, Baltimore, MD.
Sold as a McCormick product in the east; as a Schilling product in the west. Supplied in a 4-ounce foil package, this dry mix requires the addition of eggs, milk and oil. Makes extremely thin crepes when used with upside-down crepe griddles. Best crepes from this mix were made by using the batter in traditional pans.

MAKE NOW-EAT LATER

Making crepes is so much fun you may not want to stop. Fix a big batch of batter to make enough for several meals. Here are some tips on storage.

Storing batter—Batters can be stored, covered, in the refrigerator overnight. If batter separates, stir before cooking. If necessary, restore to a creamy consistency by adding 1 or 2 tablespoons of milk or flour as necessary. I do not recommend storing batter in a refrigerator longer than 24 hours. Freezing batters seems impractical because it takes longer to thaw frozen batter than to make a fresh batch.

Storing cooked crepes ready for filling—Storing crepes in a refrigerator is a tremendous time-saver. You are always ready for unexpected guests with the assurance that an elegant meal is close at hand. They may be stored in the refrigerator for 2 to 3 days if securely wrapped in foil or a plastic bag. They may be stored in the freezer up to 4 months if tightly sealed in *freezer bags*. Because crepes are delicate, especially the edges, they break easily when frozen. Therefore, after sealing the crepes in a freezer bag, it is a good idea to put the bag between two paper plates and staple them around the edges, or hold them together with transparent tape. If you have an appropriately shaped plastic container with an air-tight lid, this will work fine as a freezer container. If the plastic container does not have an air-tight lid, seal crepes in a freezer bag before putting them in the container. Bring stored crepes to room temperature before separating them. They will be easy to separate if you place foil or waxed paper between each crepe or at least between every 6 to 8 to facilitate separating and counting when ready for use. Waxed paper should be inserted after the crepes have cooled.

Storing filled crepes—As great as the home freezer is, I do not recommend it for storing some types of filled crepes. It is handy for storing dessert crepes with heavy cream fillings and other foods that you normally freeze. Some fillings do not store well in a freezer or refrigerator for extended periods, because the crepe absorbs the liquids and becomes soggy. Most fillings are far more pleasing to the palate when freshly made. If filled crepes are frozen, it's a good idea to freeze them on a cookie sheet—separated so they don't freeze together. When frozen, place them in a sealed freezer bag. Bring frozen filled crepes to room temperature before serving or heating.

Thawing or heating crepes—Use your microwave oven to thaw frozen crepes (filled or unfilled). You can also use it to heat unfilled crepes before filling and to heat filled crepes before serving.

USER'S GUIDE

One of the many advantages to crepe cookery is the variety of pans which can be used. Almost any low-sided pan with a cooking surface 6 to 8 inches in diameter will produce good crepes. A well-seasoned pan used exclusively for crepe making is not an absolute necessity. But if it is possible to season and use a pan exclusively for making crepes, consistently good results are almost guaranteed. Serious crepe makers treat such a pan like a member of the family. However, don't miss out on the enjoyment of crepes just because you don't have an honest-to-goodness crepe pan. Most kitchens have a pan similar to those shown here.

There are two types of pan seasonings—temporary and conventional or "permanent." Temporary seasoning is applying cooking oil, vegetable shortening or unsalted fat (suet) before each use and removing the oily residue after each use. "Permanent" seasoning is baking on the same kinds of oil, shortening or fat so it bonds to the metal surface. It is left on to build up with use. I do not recommend "permanent" seasoning for stainless-steel, aluminum and non-stick-coated pans or griddles. I recommend "permanent" seasoning for pans not suited for cooking other foods—especially steel and cast-iron pans or griddles.

A word about cooking temperature. I wish I could tell you an exact setting for your range. It varies with the type of pan or griddle and the space between the cooking surface and the heating element. Whether you use electricity or gas is also part of the variation. Most batters work best in most pans on *moderate* heat. Start with this temperature setting and use the water-drop test as you preheat the pan or griddle: Sprinkle a few drops of water on the cooking surface. If they merely steam without movement, the pan is not hot enough. If they vaporize almost instantly, the cooking surface is too hot. When the drops bounce and sputter or sizzle, the surface is ready. Then start cooking crepes, adjusting temperature up or down until golden-brown crepes are produced. You then have the right temperature for your crepe pan or griddle and range. Mark this setting on your range and your next cooking session will be a "cinch."

Some helpful hints! In seasoning pans, don't apply cooking oil that has previously been used to cook other foods. This can produce a sticky seasoning. In wiping hot cooking surfaces, use wadded-up paper towels so there is a safe distance between your fingers and the hot metal. Don't leave an empty pan or griddle on the heating unit longer than necessary to preheat before use. This can warp the pan; in the case of aluminum it can even melt the appliance. When cold, store the pan or griddle in an *unsealed* paper or plastic bag to protect from dust and marring of non-stick coating or seasoning.

Among the following listing of pans and griddles you will find one you like, that fits your budget. We tested every pan and griddle shown and all were satisfactory for making crepes.

User's Guide

Crepe Cooker

Crepe Master

Crepe Pan

Crepe Cooker by Associated Products Manufacturing Co., Los Angeles, CA. Upside-down griddle with 8-inch flat cooking surface. Non-stick coating on cooking surface. Wooden handle bolted to pan.

Seasoning—Wash in soapy water, rinse and dry. Conventional seasoning is not required.

Use & Care—Wipe surface with cooking oil before each use. Wooden handle location requires an extremely shallow batter dish, such as a dinner plate. Heat griddle until water-drop test indicates correct temperature. Most batters will cook best on medium heat. This griddle may tip on some burners because there is no support under the center. Wash cool pan in hot soapy water, rinse and dry. Store cold griddle in an unsealed paper or plastic bag.

Crepe Master by Atlas Metal Spinning Co., South San Francisco, CA. Upside-down griddle of spun steel with a wooden handle. Metal handle shaft welded to griddle. A separate metal utility ring raises griddle above heating unit for uniform heating. Flat cooking surface.

Seasoning—Wash with hot soapy water, rinse thoroughly and dry. Apply a light coating of cooking oil over the cooking surface with paper towels. Place utility ring over heating unit and place griddle upside down on ring. Heat on medium heat until it takes a dark-brown color. Let cool a few minutes, then recoat lightly with oil. Heat griddle again at medium temperature until it darkens a little more.

Use & Care—Preheat to cooking temperature; medium high is usually right for most batters. If batter tends to stick, coat cooking area with light film of cooking oil. After using, wipe off excess oil and batter particles with paper towels. Store cold griddle in an unsealed paper or plastic bag.

Don't use this griddle as a conventional skillet or frying pan. Direct heat on cooking surface destroys the seasoning.

Crepe Pan by Atlas Metal Spinning Co., Sou San Francisco, CA. Traditional pan of co rolled steel with wooden handle. Handle sha screws into welded-on bracket.

Seasoning—Scour thoroughly with cleanser a steel wool to remove oil. Wash with hot soap water; rinse and dry thoroughly. Place on lo heat and pour in cooking oil to cover enti bottom surface. Heat approximately 10 mi utes, tilting to cover sides with oil. Sid should be coated with oil 3 or 4 times duri heating period. Don't spill oil on heating un Pour out oil; rub inside and outside wi paper towels leaving a thin film of oil.

Use & Care—Preheat to cooking temperatur medium for most batters. Coat pan with th film of oil if needed to prevent batter fro sticking. After using and when cool, rinse wi water and softly rub with cloth or paper towe Return briefly to heating unit to dry.

Seasoning should not be removed unle rust appears. If so, repeat seasoning procedu Cleaning and reseasoning may be necessary pan is used to cook other foods.

The Perfect Crepe Pan

Contempra Automatic Crepe Maker

The Perfect Crepe Pan by Club Products Co., Division of Standex International, Cleveland, OH. Traditional aluminum crepe pan, 8-1/2-inch diameter. Flat cooking surface. Plastic handle is screw-attached. Pan kit includes measuring cup set and spatula. Rudy Stanish Omelet Pan by the same maker also works fine for crepes and is available with a non-stick surface.

Seasoning—Conventional seasoning is not required.

Use & Care—Wipe cooking surface with cooking oil and preheat to desired temperature. Most batters will cook best on medium heat. Should batter stick, apply thin coat of cooking oil periodically during cooking. After using, wash cool pan in soapy water, rinse and dry. Dishwasher will dull aluminum surface. Store cold pan in an unsealed paper or plastic bag.

Contempra Automatic Crepe Maker by Contempra Industries, Inc., New Shrewsbury, NJ. Electric upside-down griddle with slightly domed non-stick-coated cooking surface. 7-1/2-inch diameter. 650-watt heating element. Plastic base with integral heat-resistant handle. Weighs 1 lb. 8 oz.

Seasoning—Clean cooking surface with sudsy damp cloth, wipe with clean damp cloth. Conventional seasoning is not required.

Use & Care—Wipe cooking surface with cooking oil. Preheat until ready light comes on. Crepe maker is then ready to dip into batter. Light will go out while crepe is cooking, then come on again to indicate crepe is cooked. Light may signal "done" before the crepe is, but continue cooking to obtain desired degree of doneness. After use, wipe cool cooking surface with a damp paper towel. Do not immerse appliance in water. Store cold appliance in an unsealed paper or plastic bag.

User's Guide

Crepe Griddle™

French Skillet

Crepe-Plus Pan™

Crepe Griddle™ by Creative Cookware, Boulder, CO. Upside-down griddle of cast aluminum. Wood handle secured with heat- and water-resistant adhesive. Domed cooking surface.
Seasoning—Wash with mild detergent; rinse thoroughly and dry. Wipe cooking surface with vegetable oil. Place upside down on low heat for at least 30 minutes. Remove from heat and wipe surface with paper towels to remove residue.
Use & Care—Preheat to desired temperature. Most batters cook best on medium heat. If batter tends to stick, coat cooking surface with thin film of cooking oil. After using, wipe cooking surface thoroughly with paper towels. Don't wash after use as this destroys seasoning. If washing is needed to remove stains or burned particles, reseason the pan. Store cold griddle in an unsealed paper or plastic bag.

French Skillet by Cuisinarts, Inc., Greenwich, CT. Traditional pan of highly polished stainless steel; bottom is clad with thick aluminum. Compressed-wood handle is riveted to a welded-on stainless-steel shaft.
Seasoning—Wash in hot soapy water; rinse thoroughly and dry. Conventional permanent seasoning is not necessary. Coat cooking surface with vegetable shortening or oil and place on low heat. When shortening melts, wipe off excess with paper towels.
Use & Care—Preheat to proper temperature. Medium low heat is about right for most batters. After using, wash with hot soapy water, rinse and dry. Scouring powder on a damp cloth or sponge will remove stubborn stains and food residue; steel wool or metal mesh pads not recommended. Shiny outside finish can be preserved with mild liquid detergent applied with soft sponge or cloth. OK to wash in dishwasher. After washing, coat cooking surface with vegetable shortening or oil before using.
Skillet is oven-safe to 375°F (190°C), but do not put in an oven being preheated. Do not place skillet under oven broiler.

Crepe-Plus Pan™ by Ekco®-Flint®, Ekco Housewares Co., Franklin, IL. Upside-down or traditional pan of stainless steel. Heat resistant resin handle screw-attached. Crepes may be made on the outside bottom of the pan (upside-down method) or on inside bottom of pan (traditional method). Flat cooking surface.
Seasoning—Conventional or permanent seasoning is not required. Wash pan with hot soapy water, rinse thoroughly and dry. With paper towel, wipe light coat of cooking oil on selected cooking surface.
Use & Care—Preheat to proper temperature. most batters will cook best on medium heat. If sticking occurs, coat surface with cooking oil. After cooking crepes or other food, remove residue from cooking surface with plastic nylon-mesh scouring pads and kitchen cleanser or stainless-steel cleaner. Wash pan in hot soapy water, rinse and dry. When food has been cooked inside the pan, be sure the outside bottom is clean before making crepes on that surface.
Note—For this pan only, Ekco recommends adding 2 to 4 additional tablespoons of flour to the crepe batter recipes given in this book.

melet Pan

French Crepe Pan

Dip-n-flip Crepe Maker

melet Pan by Farberware®, Yonkers, NY. aditional pan. Stainless steel with a layer of uminum bonded to bottom and exterior sides. eat-resistant phenolic-resin handle is attached th rivets and a screw.

asoning—Conventional seasoning is not re- uired. Wash pan in hot soapy water to re- ove polishing compound. Rinse thoroughly id dry. Rub interior with thin coating of oking oil or solid shortening.

se & Care—Preheat to desired cooking tem- erature; for most batters medium heat is best. ould batter stick, apply thin coat of cooking periodically during cooking. After using, d when cool, wash in hot soapy water; rinse d dry. If used exclusively for crepes, washing ould clean pan. For other cooking remove ubborn spots on interior with stainless-steel ouring pads only. Keep bottom and ex- rior bright with soap-filled steel wool pad. ash in hot soapy water; rinse thoroughly d dry immediately to prevent water spots. shwasher will dull aluminum bottom and des.

Pan is oven-safe to 425°F (218°C). Do not ut pan in oven while oven is being preheated. o not place pan under broiler unit when unit on.

French Crepe Pan, made in France by Fay- mont. Traditional pan of heavy-gauge steel. Steel handle is riveted to the pan.

Seasoning—Remove protective coating on inside and outside surfaces with a paper towel soaked with rubbing alcohol, then scrub with cleanser and steel wool. Wash with hot soapy water; rinse thoroughly and dry. Place crepe pan on low heat; pour in cooking oil, about 1/8" deep. Heat pan about 10 minutes, tilting to cover sides with oil. Coat sides 3 or 4 times during heating. Don't spill oil on heating unit. Pour out oil and rub inside and outside with paper towels leaving a thin film of oil.

Use & Care—Use a pot holder because the han- dle gets hot. Preheat pan to cooking tempera- ture. Medium heat is satisfactory for most batters. Coat pan with a thin film of cooking oil occasionally to prevent sticking. After us- ing and when pan has cooled, rinse with water and softly scrub with cloth or paper towels. Return pan to heating unit briefly to dry com- pletely. Store cold pan in an unsealed paper or plastic bag.

If rust appears, scour with cleanser and steel wool. Wash in hot soapy water; rinse thoroughly, dry and reseason. This may also be necessary if used for other foods.

Dip-n-flip Crepe Maker by General Electric, Bridgeport, CT. Electric upside-down griddle with domed non-stick-coated cooking surface. 8-inch diameter, 1000-watt heating element. Plastic base with integral handle. Short "helper" handle is especially helpful for con- trolling batter coverage as you dip. Comes with a batter dish. Weighs 2 lbs. 2 oz.

Seasoning—Wash cooking surface with a damp sudsy cloth and wipe with a clean damp cloth. Conventional seasoning is not required.

Use & Care—Wipe surface with cooking oil, plug in and preheat to desired temperature— usually 3 to 5 minutes. Wipe cool cooking sur- face with a damp paper towel. Do not immerse appliance in water. Store cold appliance in an unsealed paper or plastic bag.

User's Guide

Crepe Suzette Pan

Magik Crepe Pan

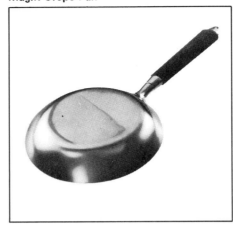

Electric Crepe Machine™

Crepe Suzette Pan by Gourmet Limited, Lombard, IL. Traditional pan. Highly polished cast-aluminum with a wooden handle. Metal shaft in handle screws into cast-in bracket.

Seasoning—Wash with detergent; rinse thoroughly and dry. Pour 1 tablespoon cooking oil in pan; tilt pan to coat all surfaces, including sloping sides. Place on low heat; add 1/2 teaspoon salt to oil. Rub cooking surface and sides with paper towels to distribute salt over surface evenly. Heat for approximately 10 minutes. Remove from heat, wipe out salt and excess oil. Pan is ready for use.

Use & Care—Preheat to cooking temperature. Most batters cook best on medium heat. At first it may be necessary to apply a thin coating of oil periodically to prevent sticking. After cooking crepes, wipe excess oil from surface and store when cool in an unsealed paper or plastic bag.

Should a residue of batter build up on the cooking surface so sticking results, scour pan with salt and paper towels.

Manufacturer recommends pan be used only for crepes.

Magik Crepe Pan by Gourmet Limited, Lombard, IL. Upside-down griddle of highly polished cast aluminum. Wooden handle's metal shaft screws into cast-in bracket. Flat cooking surface.

Seasoning—Wash in hot soapy water; rinse thoroughly and dry. Sprinkle 1/4 teaspoon salt on cooking surface. Spread melted butter or cooking oil on cooking surface with paper towel. Heat pan upside down on low for 40 minutes. Wipe excess oil and salt off griddle with paper towels.

Use & Care—Preheat to desired temperature; with most batters medium heat will be about right. If batter tends to stick, spread a thin film of butter or cooking oil over surface. After using, wipe off excess oil and batter particles with paper towels. Griddle should not need washing. Remove stains and burned batter with salt and cooking oil. Rub brisky with paper towels. Steel wool and scouring powder are not recommended. Store cold griddle in an unsealed paper or plastic bag.

Electric Crepe Machine™ by Grandinett Products, Inc., Lynwood, CA. Upside-down griddle of cast aluminum with non-stick coating. Shaft for heat-resistant resin handle is cast in. Electrically heated and thermostatically controlled. Slightly domed cooking surface. Molded plastic batter plate and spatula provided. Weighs 2 lbs. 4 oz.

Seasoning—Wipe surface with damp cloth and dry.

Use & Care—Plug into electrical outlet. If cold when connected, cooking temperature is attained in about 2 minutes, or when water drops bounce and sizzle on the cooking surface.

Relatively thin batters should be used for attractive brown-appearing crepes.

If crepes tend to stick, apply thin film of cooking oil on cooking surface with paper towels.

The handle gets too hot to hold. Use a hot pad or mitt.

After using, disconnect from electrical outlet and wipe cooking surface with paper towels. Do not immerse appliance in water. To protect the non-stick surface, store cold griddle in an unsealed paper or plastic bag.

Wonderoll Crepe Maker

Crepe Wizard

French Crepe Pan

Wonderoll Crepe Maker by Hamilton Beach Division of Scovill, Hartford, CT. Electric upside-down griddle with non-stick-coated domed 6-inch-diameter cooking surface. Metal base has screw-attached plastic handle. 700-watt heating element. Indicator light comes on during preheating and goes out to indicate correct temperature has been reached for crepe making. Weighs 2 lbs. 6 oz.

Seasoning—Wash cooking surface with damp sudsy cloth, rinse with damp clean cloth and dry. Conventional seasoning is not required.

Use & Care—Apply light coat of cooking oil to cooking surface, plug in and wait for indicator light to go out in about 3 minutes. After using, wipe cooking surface with a clean cloth. Do not immerse appliance in water. Do not use any sharp objects, abrasives or scouring pads on the non-stick surface. Store cold appliance in an unsealed paper or plastic bag.

Crepe Wizard by Hoan Products Ltd., Long Island City, NY. Upside-down griddle of steel with wooden handle. Handle's metal shaft screws into welded-on bracket. Flat cooking surface.

Seasoning—Wash with hot soapy water; rinse thoroughly and dry. Place upside down over low heat and rub cooking surface with cooking oil using paper towels. Increase heat to medium for about 10 minutes, occasionally rubbing very small amounts of oil on surface. Remove from heat and allow to cool. Wipe inside and outside with clean paper towels, leaving a thin film of oil.

Use & Care—Preheat to desired temperature; medium high for most batters. If batter tends to stick, apply thin film of cooking oil. After using, wipe away any excess oil and batter particles with paper towels.

Use this griddle only for crepes and you won't have to wash it. If you want to wash it, use warm soapy water, rinse and dry. Return to heating unit briefly for complete drying. If griddle is not washed after use, store cold griddle in an unsealed paper or plastic bag.

French Crepe Pan, made in France for Hoan Products, Ltd., Long Island, NY. Traditional pan. Steel with riveted steel handle. Package of crepe mix accompanied the pan we purchased for testing.

Seasoning—Scour with steel wool and cleanser to remove protective coating. Wash with hot soapy water; rinse thoroughly and dry. On low heat, pour about 1/8" cooking oil into pan. Heat about 10 minutes, tilting to cover sides with oil. Coat sides 2 or 3 times during heating period. Use care not to spill oil on heating unit. Using pot holder, remove from heat; pour oil out and rub inside and outside with paper towels, leaving a thin film of oil.

Use & Care—Handle gets hot, so use pot holder. Preheat to desired temperature; medium heat for most batters. It may be necessary to coat pan occasionally with a thin film of oil to prevent sticking. After using and when cool, rinse with water and softly scrub with cloth or paper towels. Return pan briefly to burner to dry.

Seasoning should not be removed unless rust appears. If this occurs, repeat seasoning procedure. This may be necessary if used to cook other foods.

User's Guide

La Crepe Complete™

Crepe Maker

Brunch Pan

La Crepe Complete™ by the Hoover Co., North Canton, OH. Traditional pan of die-cast aluminum with non-stick surface. 8-1/2-inch-diameter. Electrically heated, plug-in temperature-control unit. 800-watt heating element. Heat-resistant handle attaches with screws. Pan rests on three legs. Hoover's Mini Fry Pan is similar to this appliance.

Seasoning—Detach temperature-control unit; wash pan in hot water with mild detergent; rinse and dry thoroughly. Be sure metal electrical contacts in recess are dry. Conventional seasoning is not required. This seasoning is essential for the first use; should not be needed subsequently.

Use & Care—Spread a thin coating of cooking oil on the pan interior. Set dial at 350°F and heat for 10 minutes before making crepes. Thick batters may require a 375°F setting for best browning of crepes. After using, disconnect plug from electrical outlet, remove temperature-control unit from pan, wash pan with mild detergent. Rinse, dry and store. Do not use abrasives, strong cleaners or sharp objects on non-stick interior surface. Aluminum cleaner may be used on the exterior surface. Do not wash in dishwasher. Do not immerse temperature-control unit in water. Store in an unsealed paper or plastic bag.

Crepe Maker by Alfred E. Knobler and Co., Inc., Moonachie, NJ. Upside-down griddle of aluminum with a wooden handle. Handle's metal shaft screws into cast-in bracket. Dome-shaped cooking surface.

Seasoning—Wash in hot soapy water; rinse thoroughly and dry. Wipe cooking surface with cooking oil using paper towels. Place upside down on low heat for 30 minutes. Repeat applications of oil during heating process if part of surface appears to be drying. Wipe off excess oil with paper towels.

Use & Care—Preheat to desired temperature; moderate heat for most batters. If batter tends to stick, apply thin film of cooking oil as needed. After using, wipe off excess oil and batter particles with paper towels.

Washing should not be required. If desired, use mild detergent; rinse and dry. Reseasoning may be necessary after washing. If not washed after use, store cold griddle in an unsealed paper or plastic bag.

If scouring is needed, try removing stains with salt and cooking oil. Rub briskly with paper towels. Scour with steel wool or cleansers only as a last resort; reseasoning is required.

Brunch Pan by Leyse Aluminum Company, Kewaunee, WI. Traditional pan of aluminum has a metal handle attached with rivets.

Seasoning—Wash with hot soapy water; rinse thoroughly and dry. Place on low heat and pour cooking oil to very near top of pan. Heat on low for 3 hours. Don't spill oil on heating unit. Pour out oil and wipe interior of pan with paper towels, leaving a thin film of oil. Pan is ready for use.

Use & Care—Preheat to desired temperature; for most batters use medium heat. Handle gets hot so use a pot holder. If batter tends to stick, apply thin film of cooking oil. After using and when cool, wipe pan with damp cloth and rub with salt. Remove salt with paper towel before storing. Store cold pan in an unsealed paper or plastic bag.

Saute-Fry Pan

Crepes 'N Things™

Nordic Ware® Electric Crepe Maker

Saute-Fry Pan by Mirro Aluminum Co., Manitowoc, WI. Two similar traditional pans are marketed under the same name. Both aluminum with heat-resistant resin handle. One has non-stick interior coating of black Teflon II®, other is white Teflon II®. Instructions apply to both models.

Seasoning—Non-stick coating eliminates conventional seasoning. Wash in dishwasher or hot soapy water; rinse and dry.

Use & Care—Coat interior with oil. Preheat to desired temperature. Most batters work best with medium heat. After use, wash with hot soapy water; rinse thoroughly and dry. OK to wash in dishwasher. Don't use steel wool or scouring powder, use only nylon or plastic cleaning aids. Store cold pan in an unsealed paper or plastic bag.

Use only plastic, nylon, rubber, wood or non-stick coated spatulas on pan's surface as metal ones will mar Teflon® coating.

With prolonged use, minor staining of the non-stick material may occur. Stain may be lightened following procedure described in discussion of French Skillet on Page 36.

Crepes 'N Things™ by Nordic Ware®, Northland Aluminum Co., Minneapolis, MN. Upside-down griddle of cast aluminum with non-stick coating. Wood handle. Notched handle bracket fits over the edge of a shallow batter pan to simplify even (level) dipping and use of batter. Highly domed cooking surface.

Seasoning—Wash with mild soap or detergent in hot water; rinse thoroughly and dry.

Use & Care—Coat cooking surface with oil. Preheat to cooking temperature. For most batters, medium heat is about right. If batter tends to stick, coat cooking surface lightly with cooking oil. After using wipe with paper towels. Store cold griddle in an unsealed paper or plastic bag.

Nordic Ware® Electric Crepe Maker by Northland aluminum Products, Minneapolis, MN. Electric upside-down griddle with non-stick-coated, domed 8-inch-diameter cooking surface. Plastic base with integral handle. 750-watt heating element. Indicator light comes on when correct temperature for crepe making is attained. Weighs 2 lbs. 6 oz.

Seasoning—Wipe off cooking surface with damp sudsy cloth. Rinse with clean damp cloth and dry. Conventional seasoning is not required.

Use & Care—Lightly coat cooking surface with oil. Plug in and wait for light to come on before making crepes. Wash cool appliance with damp sudsy cloth, then with clean damp cloth. Do not immerse in water. Do not use abrasive cleaners, scouring pads or sharp objects on the non-stick surface. Store cold appliance in an unsealed paper or plastic bag.

User's Guide

French Skillet

Master Chef Electric Crepe Maker

Electric Create-a-Crepe

French Skillet by Nordic Ware® Northland Aluminum Products, Inc., Minneapolis, MN. Traditional pan. Aluminum with non-stick coating on cooking surface. Heat-resistant resin handle is fastened with screws.

Seasoning—Because of the non-stick surface, conventional seasoning is not necessary. Wash skillet in hot soapy water; rinse thoroughly and dry.

Use & Care—Coat cooking surface with oil. Pre-heat skillet to cooking temperature; medium heat is usually best. If used exclusively for crepes, you may wipe out excess oil with paper towels rather than washing the utensil. After cooking other foods, wash with hot soapy water; rinse and dry. Use only nylon or plastic cleaning aids if scouring becomes necessary. Store cool pan in an unsealed paper or plastic bag.

Use only plastic, nylon, rubber, wood or non-stick coated spatulas; metal will mar the non-stick coating.

Use may discolor the coating. This will not affect performance. Staining may be lightened by preparing a heaping tablespoon baking soda and 1/3 cup liquid household bleach in 1 cup water. Heat solution in skillet to boil; simmer 5 minutes. Wash with hot soapy water; rinse thoroughly and dry. Wipe interior with light coat of oil or solid shortening.

Master Chef Electric Crepe Maker by Northern Electric Co., Chicago, IL. Electric upside-down griddle with non-stick-coated 8-inch-diameter domed cooking surface. Plastic base includes handle. Indicator light turns on when unit is ready to make crepes. 750-watt heating element. Weighs 2 lbs. 2 oz.

Seasoning—Wipe cooking surface with a damp sudsy cloth, wipe with a clean damp cloth and dry. Conventional seasoning is not required.

Use & Care—Apply light coat of cooking oil to cooking surface. Plug in unit and wait for indicator light to turn on, which takes about 2 minutes. Unit is then ready to make crepes. After using, let cool, and wipe off cooking surface with a clean cloth. Do not immerse in water. Do not use any scouring pads, sharp objects or abrasive cleaners on the non-stick surface. Store cold appliance in an unsealed paper or plastic bag.

Electric Create-a-Crepe by Osrow Products Co., Glen Cove, NY. Electric upside-down griddle with non-stick-coated, 8-inch-diameter, domed cooking surface. Heat-resistant plastic handle is screw-attached. 600-watt heating element. Spatula and dipping dish included. Weighs 1 lb. 14 oz.

Seasoning—Wipe cooking surface with damp sudsy cloth. Rinse with clean dampened cloth. Conventional seasoning is not required.

Use & Care—Wipe cooking surface with a light coating of cooking oil. Plug in and allow to preheat for about 5 minutes before making crepes. Wipe cooled cooking surface with paper towel after use. Do not immerse appliance in water. Store appliance in an unsealed plastic or paper bag.

Creperie™

French Skillet

Crepe Magician™

Creperie™ **by Oster Corporation, Milwaukee, WI.** Electric upside-down griddle with non-stick, domed 7-1/2-inch-diameter cooking surface. Plastic base with integral heat-resistant handle. Weighs 2 lbs. 4 oz.

Seasoning—Wash cooking surface with cloth or paper towel dampened in hot soapy water. Rinse by wiping with clean dampened cloth and dry. Conventional seasoning is not required.

Use & Care—Wipe surface with cooking oil. Plug into electrical outlet and heat for 3 minutes or until desired temperature is attained. Let unit cool before wiping cooking surface with a damp paper towel. Do not immerse appliance in water. Store appliance in an unsealed paper or plastic bag.

French Skillet by Oster™ **distributed by Marvelle Gourmet Cookware, Escondido, CA.** Traditional pan of aluminum with non-stick coating. Exterior is black porcelain. Heat-resistant resin handle is screw-attached.

Seasoning—Conventional or permanent seasoning is not needed. Wash in hot soapy water; rinse thoroughly and dry.

Use & Care—Coat cooking surface with oil. Most batters cook best on medium heat. Preheat to cooking temperature. Washable in dishwasher. To scour, use nylon or plastic cleaning aids only. Store cold pan in an unsealed paper or plastic bag.

Use only plastic, nylon, rubber, wood or non-stick coated spatulas; metal mars skillet's non-stick surface. Handle is oven-safe to 425°F (218°C), but skillet should not be put in oven being preheated. Do not use under oven broiler. Non-stick surface may eventually stain, but this will not affect performance. Lighten stain by procedure for French Skillet on Page 36.

Crepe Magician™ **by Popeil®, Popeil Brothers, Inc., Chicago, IL.** Traditional pan of die-cast aluminum with Teflon® non-stick coating on cooking surface. Heat-resistant resin handle screw-attached to cast-in bracket. Plastic freezer storage container for about 25 crepes is provided with pan.

Seasoning—Wipe with damp cloth.

Use & Care—Coat cooking surface with oil. Preheat to cooking temperature. Medium heat works best for most batters. After using, wipe out excess oil with paper towels. Store cold pan in an unsealed paper or plastic bag. If used for cooking other foods (not recommended), wash with hot soapy water; rinse thoroughly and dry. Reseason pan before cooking crepes.

User's Guide

Crepe Suzette Pan

Limited Edition Crepe Pan

Omelet Pan

Revere Ware® Crepe Suzette Pan by Revere Copper and Brass, Inc., Clinton, IL. Finishing pan with stainless-steel interior, copper exterior. Brass handle is riveted to the pan.

Use & Care—This specialized pan can be used to flame suzettes and other crepes; or to heat and, in some instances, make sauces in which crepes are dipped. Flat, wide bottom facilitates use on a chafing-dish stand. Attractive color complements table setting.

The new pan has a transparent protective coating on the copper surface. Before cooking, remove by immersing the pan in hot water for a few minutes until the coating turns "milky." Then scratch the coating at the edge of the pan with your fingernail and it will peel off easily.

After using, wash pan in hot soapy water; rinse and dry thoroughly. If food is burned on the inner surface, use a nylon, plastic or fine steel wool pad to scour. Remove discoloration on the stainless-steel and brass surfaces with a copper cleaner. After using cleaner, wash pan in hot soapy water; rinse and dry immediately. If stored with other utensils, store in an unsealed paper or plastic bag to avoid scratching the copper finish.

Revere Ware® Limited Edition Crepe Pan by Revere Copper & Brass, Inc., Clinton, IL. Traditional 8-1/2-inch pan is solid copper outside for even heat distribution. Stainless-steel interior has flat cooking surface. Solid-brass handle is riveted to pan.

Seasoning—Protective finish must be removed before pan is used for cooking. Maker claims finish will come off if you immerse pan in hot water until surface turns "milky." Scratch surface with a fingernail and peel coating off. We had to use lacquer thinner to remove the coating. Stainless-steel cooking surface does not require conventional seasoning.

Use & Care—Coat cooking surface with cooking oil and preheat pan to desired temperature. Most batters cook best on medium heat. Wash in hot suds. Fine steel wool can be used on stainless-steel interior surface to remove stubborn bits of food. Exterior should only be cleaned with copper cleaner and a cloth to avoid scratching surface. Dishwasher will dull the surfaces. Store cold pan in an unsealed paper or plastic bag.

Revere Ware® Omelet Pan by Revere Copper and Brass, Inc., Clinton, IL. Traditional pan. Stainless-steel with copper-clad bottom. Support for heat-resistant phenolic-resin handle is welded to pan.

Seasoning—Stainless-steel surface does not require conventional seasoning. Wash pan with hot soapy water; rinse thoroughly and dry.

Use & Care—Apply a thin coating of cooking oil to cooking surface. Preheat to cooking temperature; medium heat for most batters. If batter sticks, coat cooking surface with thin film of oil as necessary. After using and when cool, wash with hot soapy water; rinse thoroughly and dry with clean, soft towel. If used exclusively for crepes, washing should clean pan. If used for other foods, soak in water before washing.

Use good copper cleaner to remove discoloration from bottom surface and to keep stainless steel bright and shiny. Wash and dry immediately with clean, soft towel. Store pan in an unsealed paper or plastic bag to protect the copper finish.

'sieur Crepe

T-Fal® Skillet

Dinner Crepe Pan

'sieur Crepe by Sunbeam, Oakbrook, IL. Electric upside-down griddle with separate 50-watt heating base. Heat-resistant plastic handle is user-attached with screws to a bracket riveted to griddle. Non-stick-coated flat cooking surface is 7-3/4-inch diameter. Griddle can be inverted and used as a traditional crepe pan for frying. Interior surface is also non-stick coated. Heating base has variable temperature control for crepes or frying.

Seasoning—Wash in warm soapy water with soft cloth. Rinse and dry. Conventional seasoning not required.

Use & Care—Set heat control to low end of crepe range. Lightly brush cooking oil onto cooking surface. Do not apply oil to heating base. Place griddle with domed surface onto heating base and preheat 4 minutes. Longer reheating times make the griddle too hot so first crepe will be lost by slipping back into the batter. After dipping, invert the griddle and put it back on the heating base until crepe is done—usually about 1 to 1-1/2 minutes.

If you want browner crepes, use a higher heat setting.

Clean cool griddle in warm soapy water. Rinse and dry. Do not use any abrasives, cleaning pads or sharp objects on griddle or interior cooking surfaces. Store griddle in a plastic bag. Wipe outside of cool base with a damp cloth and dry. Do not immerse heating base in water. Cord wraps around base for storage.

T-Fal® Skillet, made in France for T-Fal Housewares, Belleville, NJ. Traditional pan. Aluminum with a non-stick coating on cooking surface. Handle is heat-resistant resin, attached with a screw.

Seasoning—Conventional seasoning not required. Wash in hot soapy water. Rinse thoroughly and dry.

Use & Care—Coat inside surface with cooking oil. Preheat to cooking temperature; medium heat for most batters. If skillet is used exclusively for crepes, wipe out excess oil with paper towels after use. For other cooking, wash in dishwasher or hot soapy water. Rinse thoroughly and dry. Don't use steel wool or scouring powder. Store cool pan in an unsealed paper or plastic bag.

Use only plastic, nylon, rubber, wood or non-stick coated spatulas; metal will scratch the non-stick coating.

Dinner Crepe Pan by Taylor and Ng, San Francisco, CA. Traditional pan. Cold-rolled steel with a wooden handle. Metal handle shaft screws into metal bracket welded to pan.

Seasoning—Scrub thoroughly with cleanser, steel wool and hot water to remove oil coating. Wash with warm soapy water; rinse thoroughly and dry. Place on low heat and pour 1/8" to 1/4" of cooking oil in pan. Heat approximately 10 minutes, tilting to cover the sloping sides with oil. Sides should be covered 3 or 4 times during the heating process. Use care not to spill oil on burner. Remove from burner; pour out oil and wipe seasoned surface, then outside surface, with paper towels leaving a thin oil film.

Use & Care—Preheat pan to cooking temperature. Most batters work best on medium heat. At first it may be necessary to apply a thin coat of oil periodically to prevent sticking. After making crepes, and when pan is cool, rinse with water and softly scrub with cloth or paper towel. Return briefly to burner to dry. Rub with a little oil; cool and store.

Removing seasoning is not recommended unless rusting occurs. Should rust appear, repeat seasoning procedure. Do not wash in dishwasher.

Store in an unsealed paper or plastic bag.

User's Guide

The Crepe Maker

Chef Skillet

Crepe-ette Master

The Crepe Maker by Taylor and Ng, San Francisco, CA. Upside-down griddle of cold-rolled steel with wooden handle. Handle's metal shaft screws into welded-on bracket. Domed cooking surface.

Seasoning—Scour thoroughly with cleanser, steel wool and hot water to remove protective coating. Wash with hot soapy water; rinse thoroughly and dry. Place upside down over low heat and rub cooking oil over surface with paper towels. Increase heat to medium for about 10 minutes, occasionally rubbing very small amounts of cooking oil on surface. Remove from heat and allow to cool. Wipe inside and out with clean paper towels, leaving a thin oil film.

Use & Care—Preheat to desired temperature; medium high for most batters. If batter tends to stick, apply a thin film of cooking oil. This griddle may tip on some burners because there is no support under the center. After using wipe away any excess oil and batter particles with paper towels.

Use only for crepe making and no washing will be needed. To wash, use warm soapy water; rinse and dry. Return to heating unit briefly for complete drying. If not washed after use, store cold griddle in an unsealed paper or plastic bag. If scoured with abrasive cleaning aids to remove rust, reseasoning is necessary.

Chef Skillet by Griswold®, Wagner Mfg. Co., Sidney, OH. Traditional pan. One-piece cast-iron skillet and handle.

Seasoning—Remove label by placing skillet on burner and heating slightly. With dry cloth or paper towel, rub off label. Wash in hot soapy water; rinse and dry thoroughly. Skillet has been preseasoned by manufacturer, but for best results should be seasoned again before use. Coat inside of skillet with unsalted fat (preferably suet) or solid vegetable shortening and place in 300°F (149°C) oven for two hours. Remove from oven with pot holder and wipe out excess fat with paper towels. Pan is ready for use.

Use & Care—Preheat skillet to cooking temperature. Most batters cook on medium heat. Handle gets hot, so use a pot holder. At first it may be necessary to apply a very thin coat of shortening periodically to prevent sticking. After use and when cool, wash in warm soapy water; rinse and dry thoroughly. If desired, coat inside of skillet with light film of unsalted shortening. Store in a warm dry place.

If rust forms or it becomes absolutely necessary to scour skillet, reseason before using. Do not wash in dishwasher.

Crepe-ette Master by Wagner Ware Division of General Housewares, Terre Haute, IN. Cast-iron griddle, 8-1/2-inch diameter. Flat cooking surface to make 6-1/4-inch crepes. Griddle casting includes handle. Comes with handy batter dipper.

Seasoning—Heat on medium heat to melt glue attaching label. Pull label off and rub surface with a dry cloth to remove any remaining glue. Coat entire griddle, front and back, with cooking oil and heat in 375°F oven for 30 minutes.

Use & Care—Wipe lightly with cooking oil and preheat to desired temperature. Most batters cook best on medium heat. Discard first two crepes as they may absorb excessive oil. After using, wipe cool griddle with a clean dry cloth and store griddle in an unsealed paper bag. Do not immerse this griddle in water or wash it in a dishwasher. Its operation relies on "permanent" seasoning.

aute-Pan	Crepe Pan Kit	Crepe Queen

aute-Pan by Wear-Ever, Chillicothe, OH. Tradi-onal aluminum crepe pan, 8-inch diameter. lat cooking surface. Metal handle attached ith rivets.

easoning—Wash in hot soapy water, rub nterior with steel wool or scouring pad, rinse nd dry. Conventional seasoning not required.

Ise & Care—Lightly coat with cooking oil, reheat to desired temperature. Most batters ill cook best on medium heat. Should batter tick, apply thin coat of cooking oil periodical-y during cooking. After using, wash in hot oapy water, rinse and dry. Dishwasher will ull aluminum surface.

Crepe Pan Kit by the West Bend Company, West Bend, WI. Traditional aluminum pan with non-stick coating on flat interior cooking surface. Exterior is porcelain finish. Handle is attached onto a bracket which is riveted to the 10-inch-diameter pan. Kit includes a measuring cup.

Seasoning—Wash in hot soapy water, rinse and dry. Conventional seasoning not required.

Use & Care—Wipe interior of pan with cooking oil and preheat to desired temperature. Most batters cook best on medium heat. After using, let cool, then wash in soapy water. Pan may also be washed in dishwasher. Do not use any abbrasives, scouring pads or sharp objects on non-stick surface. Pan can be used in the oven at temperatures to 350°F. Do not use in an oven which is being preheated. Store cold pan in an unsealed paper or plastic bag.

Crepe Queen by Silver Shield Cookware, (Westminster Export Co., Inc.), Atlanta, GA. Traditional aluminum crepe pan, 8-inch-diameter, flat, non-stick-coated cooking surface. Plastic screw-on handle is oven-proof to 375°F. Also available in 10- and 12-inch sizes.

Seasoning—Wash in hot soapy water, rinse and dry.

Use & Care—Coat pan interior with cooking oil. Preheat pan to desired temperature. Most batters will cook best on medium heat. Wash pan in hot sudsy water or dishwasher after use. Store in an unsealed paper or plastic bag. Dishwasher will dull pan exterior.

PARAPHERNALIA & STUFF

You probably already have all or most of the things you need to make crepes: Mixing bowl, whisk or wooden spoon—or a kitchen blender.

A pan or skillet about 6- to 8-inch diameter and any suitable spatula can make excellent crepes.

Upside-down griddles are dipped into a shallow container of batter. If yours didn't come with a dipping plate, a 9-inch pie plate or a dinner plate works fine.

When stacking crepes, a large pan lid is handy to cover and keep them moist.

Experience and experimentation—used with a little kitchen know-how—will solve most problems in cooking crepes. Some problems are unique to certain types of batter or cooking pan. Most are solved by use of correct heating temperatures, good batter recipes that work in any type of pan, and proper use of cooking implements. Here are some problems and solutions.

HOW TO KNOW WHEN YOU ARE DOING IT RIGHT

PROBLEM	CAUSE	CURE
Too many bubbles.	Beating batter mixture at too high speed in mixer or blender.	Mix at lower speed.
	Cooking batter immediately after mixing.	Let batter stand at least 1 hour.
Small holes in center of crepe.	Heat build-up under batter.	With spoon or spatula, drip small amount of batter over holes in crepe while cooking.
Batter falls off upside-down griddle back into dipping plate.	Crepe griddle too hot.	Lower cooking temperature.
	Too much oil on griddle.	Wipe off excess oil.
	Griddle left in batter too long.	Dip faster.
	Suction due to jerking up crepe griddle after dipping.	Don't jerk out of batter.
Crepes have lacy pattern.	Typical of first and sometimes second crepe. Crepes OK after that.	Discard first and second crepe.
	Batter too thin.	Mix 1 or 2 tablespoons flour into batter.
Batter sticks to pan.	Pan not oiled or seasoned correctly.	Follow directions for oiling and seasoning.
	Heat too low.	Increase heat.
Edges of crepe are very crisp and tend to crack.	Batter too thin.	Mix 1 or 2 tablespoons flour into batter.
	Pan too hot.	Decrease heat.
Batter runs down sides of upside-down griddle.	Batter too thin.	Mix 1 or 2 tablespoons flour into batter.
	Griddle not hot enough.	Increase heat.
Batter won't swirl in traditional pan.	Batter too thick.	Mix 1 or 2 tablespoons milk or water into batter.
Crepes aren't round.	Uneven dipping with upside-down griddle.	Hold level while dipping.
	Batter not swirled in traditional pan.	Lift pan off heat and carefully swirl batter.

MENU IDEAS

Serve crepes around the clock. Let them come to your rescue for good and varied menus throughout the day—planned meals *and* impromptu snacks. Main-dish crepes combine some type of sauce or topping; with a meat, poultry, cheese, egg or seafood filling—sometimes with a vegetable, too. Many of these are meals in themselves. You will find crepe menus are shorter than most traditional menus because of the many ingredients in the filled crepe.

BREAKFAST
Farm Style
Grapefruit Halves
Dairyland Scrambled Egg Crepes
Country Sausage
Home Fried Potatoes

City Style
Spicy Tomato Juice
Deviled Ham & Egg Crepes
Quick Cinnamon Rolls

LUNCH
Anniversary Celebration
Peaches in Champagne
Eggs Benedict Crepes
Miniature Danish Rolls
Soft Butter

On the Patio
Fresh Pineapple with Strawberries
Eggs Continental
Broiled Tomato Halves
Dill Bread with Butter

South of the Border
Margaritas
Salted Sunflower Seeds
Huevos Rancheros Crepes
Sliced Avocado & Orange Salad
Oil & Vinegar Dressing

Family Get-together
Fresh Orange Juice
Broiled Ham Slices
Scrambled Eggs
Strudel-Style Apple Crepes

Out-of-Town Guests
Canteloupe with Blueberries
Brunch Special
Broiled Bacon
Cheese Rolls

Far East Intrigue
Sliced Bananas & Oranges
Egg Crepes, East Indian Style
Peanuts, Coconuts, Pineapple Wedges & Kumquats

Old Heidelberg Style
Rathskeller Crepes
Potato Cakes
Sliced Dill Pickles
Beer
Apple Crisp

Dressed-up Sandwich
Ham-Stuffed Crepes
Potato Chips
Tomato Aspic
Angel Food Cake

Aloha!
Fresh Papaya Slices with Lime
Chicken Salad
Desert Isle Crepewich
Pineapple Sherbet

Bridge Club Special
Crab Crepewiches
Sliced Tomatoes & Cucumbers
Orange Chiffon Cake

DINNER
French Connection
Paté Provencale—Crackers
Parisienne Chicken Crepes
Buttered Baby Peas & Onions
Endive Salad
French Pastries

Male Favorite
Deviled Steak Crepes
Potato Buds
Onion Rings
Mixed Greens with Roquefort Dressing
Apple Pie with Cheese

The Ultimate
Lobster Newburg Crepes
Buttered Asparagus Spears
Avocado & Artichoke Salad
Baked Lemon Meringues

Tuna Clipper
Tuna with Herb Sauce
Buttered Summer Squash
Tomato Wedges
Deep-Dish Blueberry Pie

Roman Influence
Antipasto
Cannelloni Style Crepes
Broccoli with Lemon
Spumoni Ice Cream

Tahitian Paradise
Polynesian Crepes
Glazed Acorn Squash
Papaya, Mandarin Orange & Coconut Salad
Banana Cream Tarts

SNACK TIME
Teen Get-together
Pizza Crepes
Carrot & Celery Sticks
Pickles & Olives
Ice Cream Bars
Soft Drinks

After the Game
Sloppy Joe Crepes
Buttered Green Beans
Carrot Cole Slaw
Double Chocolate Brownies

Midnight Supper
Roast Beef Sandwiches
Mixed Green Salad
Flaming Berry Creams
Irish Coffee

Monday Night Football
Guacamole—Taco Chips
Beef & Bean Burrito
Spanish Rice
Lime Sherbet

Holiday Party
Appetizer Dippin' Chips
Cheese Spread
Smoked Salmon Rolls
Party Wedges
Mixed Nuts
Wine Fruit Punch

POULTRY

Chicken is a very popular ingredient of dinner crepes. How else can you produce an elegant main dish serving six to eight people, using only two cups of cooked chicken? And it's sophisticated too. There's *Curry of Chicken Breast Crepes* reminiscent of India, *Parisiene Chicken Crepes* with a rich French sauce, *Chicken Saltimbocca* with an Italian accent and *Chicken or Turkey Enchilada* to represent Mexico.

Of course you can substitute chicken for turkey and vice versa. Concerned about food costs? Try my budget stretcher. Whenever chicken or turkey is moderately priced, I buy more than I need at the moment. For example, I'll buy an extra package of turkey parts or a larger turkey than I need, extra chicken parts or an additional whole chicken. Then I cook the extra poultry, bone it, cut it up, and freeze it in packages of about 1 cup per package. That way I can thaw one or more packages at a time to make crepes. This is not only a money-saver, but also a real convenience—a quick and easy way to fix a delectable main dish without a trip to the store.

Some recipes call for specific parts of chicken such as breasts or thighs. Feel free to substitute cut up whole chicken (cooked and boned) or other parts if that is more convenient. Chicken thighs and breasts provide more actual meat per pound but they are often more expensive. You'll have to balance cost and convenience when deciding which is best for you.

Poultry is an American favorite. If you don't know the taste preferences of your guests, you can usually be sure they'll enjoy chicken. The sky's the limit for flavor combinations with poultry. It is compatible with many kinds of cheeses, sour cream and other dairy products used in crepe sauces. Also, I combine it with broccoli or spinach in several recipes. You might like to vary these with the addition of some of *your* favorite vegetables.

For the cooked crepes to use with poultry, you have an almost unlimited choice. *All-Purpose Crepes* are the most popular, and provide the most likely shell for poultry recipes. However, don't overlook *Herb Batter* for a little extra flavor or the *Cornmeal Batter* for a "Down South" combination—or mix and match your own.

Chicken Elegante

Delicious rich sauce blends perfectly with chicken!

2 tablespoons butter
1 clove garlic, crushed
3 lbs. chicken thighs and/or breasts
1 teaspoon salt
1/8 teaspoon white pepper
1/2 cup chicken broth or bouillon

1/2 cup dry white wine
1 tablespoon minced parsley
1/2 teaspoon crushed tarragon leaves
1 cup heavy cream
3 egg yolks
16 warm cooked crepes

In large skillet, melt butter with garlic. Add chicken, salt, pepper, broth, wine, parsley, and tarragon. Cover and cook until chicken is very tender. Remove chicken from broth; cool slightly. Remove bones and cut meat into small pieces. Set aside and keep warm. Meanwhile, stir cream into broth. Beat egg yolks. Add several tablespoons hot broth to eggs; then stir this mixture into remaining broth. Cook over low heat, beating constantly with a whisk until slightly thickened. Fill each warm cooked crepe with about 1/4 cup of cooked chicken. Spoon about one tablespoon sauce onto each crepe; fold over. Pour remaining sauce over filled crepes. Serve hot. Makes 16 crepes.

Parisienne Chicken Crepes

Delectable, rich chicken crepes with a French accent.

2 tablespoons butter
2 tablespoons flour
1 cup chicken bouillon or broth
1/4 teaspoon salt
1/2 cup sliced fresh mushrooms

1 egg yolk
1/4 cup heavy cream
1 cup cooked diced chicken or turkey
6 to 8 cooked crepes
1/4 cup grated Swiss cheese

Melt butter in saucepan. Blend in flour. Then add bouillon and salt; stir and cook over moderate heat about 2 minutes or until thickened. Stir in mushrooms; cook for 1 minute. Remove from heat. Mix egg yolk with cream. Stir small amount of hot mixture into egg yolk. Then stir egg mixture into saucepan. Cook over low heat for another minute. Stir in chicken or turkey. In large shallow baking dish, fill crepes with chicken mixture; fold over. Sprinkle with cheese. Cover and heat in 350°F (177°C) oven for 15 to 20 minutes. Makes 6 to 8 crepes.

Chicken Divan Crepes

Rich, but SO good!

1/4 cup butter
1/4 cup flour
2 cups chicken broth
2 teaspoons Worcestershire sauce
3 cups grated cheddar cheese

2 cups dairy sour cream
2 (10-oz.) pkgs. frozen broccoli spears or
   1 1/2 lbs. broccoli, cooked and drained
2 cups chopped cooked chicken
12 cooked crepes

Over medium heat, melt butter in small saucepan. Stir in flour and cook until bubbly. Add broth and Worcestershire sauce; cook, stirring until thickened. Add 2 cups cheese. Empty sour cream into medium bowl; gradually add hot cheese sauce, stirring constantly. In large shallow baking dish, place cooked broccoli and cooked chicken on each crepe. Spoon 1 tablespoon sauce over each. Fold crepes over. Pour remaining sauce over all. Sprinkle with remaining cup of cheese. Cover and heat in 350°F (177°C) oven for 20 to 30 minutes. Makes 12 crepes.

Curry of Chicken Breast Crepes

Just the right touch of curry.

1/4 cup chopped onion
1/4 cup chopped celery
1/4 cup butter
1/2 teaspoon salt
1 tablespoon curry powder
1/4 cup flour

1 cup milk or light cream
1 1/2 cups chicken broth or bouillon
1 tablespoon sherry
3 cups chopped cooked chicken
10 cooked crepes
1/3 cup grated Parmesan cheese

Sauté onions and celery in butter several minutes; mix in salt and curry powder. Add flour; cook until bubbly. Pour in milk and broth; cook on low heat, stirring until smooth and thick. Remove from heat; add sherry. Divide sauce in half; add chicken to half the sauce. Spoon about 3 tablespoons of chicken mixture onto center of each crepe; fold over. Place crepes in large shallow baking pan and pour remaining sauce over all. Sprinkle with Parmesan cheese. Heat in 350°F (177°C) oven for 20 to 25 minutes. Makes 10 crepes.

Chicken Divan Crepes

Poulet Albert Crepes

If you're an "orange" enthusiast, this one is for you.

2 tablespoons melted butter
2 lbs. chicken breasts and thighs
1 cup orange juice
1 tablespoon grated orange peel
1/2 teaspoon salt
1/8 teaspoon pepper
2 teaspoons finely chopped crystalline ginger

1/2 teaspoon garlic powder
1 teaspoon onion powder
1/4 cup orange liqueur
2 tablespoons cornstarch
1 tablespoon cold water
16 cooked crepes

In roasting pan, spoon melted butter over chicken. In mixing bowl, combine orange juice, peel, salt, pepper, ginger, garlic and onion powder, and orange liqueur; pour over chicken. Cover and bake in 350°F (177°C) oven for 45 minutes or until chicken is done. Remove chicken from oven; skin, bone, and cut chicken into thin slivers. Pour sauce from roasting pan into medium saucepan. Dissolve cornstarch in water; add to sauce. Cook over medium heat, stirring constantly until thickened. Place about 2 tablespoons chicken and 1 tablespoon sauce in center of each crepe; fold over. Place in shallow baking pan. Spoon remaining sauce over all. Bake at 350°F (177°C) for 10 to 15 minutes. Makes 16 crepes.

Cashew Chicken Crepes

Chinese fortune cookie says, "You'll like this!"

3 tablespoons butter or cooking oil
1/2 cup cashew nuts, coarsely chopped
2 cups uncooked chicken or turkey, cut into
   thin slivers
1 cup thinly sliced cauliflower or broccoli
4 green onions, sliced

1 cup chicken bouillon
1 tablespoon cornstarch
2 tablespoons soy sauce
10 warm cooked crepes
1 orange, peeled and sliced

In large skillet, heat butter or oil; add cashews and cook over medium-high heat, stirring until nuts are lightly toasted. Remove nuts from pan, leaving butter or oil. Stir in chicken and cauliflower or broccoli; cook about 5 minutes, stirring constantly. Add onions and bouillon. Cover and cook several minutes. Dissolve cornstarch in soy sauce; stir into chicken mixture. Cook, stirring until thickened. Add toasted cashews. Fill warm crepes. Garnish with orange slices. Makes 10 crepes.

Try Chinese pea pods instead of cauliflower or broccoli; add them the last couple of minutes when cooking the chicken.

Chicken Crepes, Normandy

An interesting combination with herbs and cider.

2 whole chicken breasts
2 tablespoons butter
1/2 teaspoon seasoned salt
1 onion, minced
2 teaspoons chopped parsley
1/8 teaspoon thyme

1/8 teaspoon rosemary
2/3 cup apple cider
1 cup light cream
2 tablespoons cornstarch
12 or 13 warm cooked crepes

Bone and skin chicken; cut into small strips. Melt butter in skillet. Add chicken; sauté several minutes. Stir in seasoned salt, onion, parsley, thyme, rosemary, and cider. Cover and simmer about 10 minutes or until chicken is tender. Remove chicken from cider mixture; keep chicken warm. Combine cream with cornstarch; add to cider mixture. Cook on low heat, stirring constantly until thickened. Place about 2 tablespoons cooked chicken and 1 tablespoon sauce on each warm crepe; roll up. Put into shallow serving dish. Spoon remaining sauce over all. Serve immediately. Makes 12 or 13 crepes.

Quick Chicken & Broccoli Crepes

Use frozen broccoli and canned soup to make these on a moment's notice.

1 (10-oz.) pkg. frozen chopped broccoli
1 (10 3/4-oz.) can condensed cream of chicken
  soup
1/2 teaspoon Worcestershire sauce
1/3 cup grated Parmesan cheese

2 cups cooked slivered chicken or turkey
14 to 16 cooked crepes
1/3 cup mayonnaise
1 tablespoon milk
1/4 cup grated Parmesan cheese

Cook broccoli according to package directions; drain thoroughly. Combine with condensed soup, Worcestershire sauce, 1/3 cup cheese, and chicken. Fill crepes with chicken mixture; roll up and place in shallow baking pan. Combine mayonnaise with milk; spread over crepes. Sprinkle with 1/4 cup cheese. Broil until bubbly. Makes 14 to 16 crepes.

Chicken Liver Bearnaise Crepes

Glamorize chicken livers with a quick 'n easy Hollandaise mix.

1 lb. chicken livers
1/4 cup butter
2 tablespoons finely chopped onion
2 tablespoons dry white wine

1 tablespoon lemon juice
1/2 teaspoon seasoned salt
1/8 teaspoon marjoram
6 to 8 cooked crepes

Sauce:
1 (1 1/8-oz.) envelope Hollandaise sauce mix
1 cup milk
2 tablespoons chopped green onions

1/2 teaspoon dried, crushed tarragon
1/4 teaspoon dried, crushed chervil

Cut livers into small chunks. Melt butter in skillet; add chicken livers and onion. Sauté several minutes. Stir in wine, lemon juice, seasoned salt, and marjoram. Simmer 2 or 3 minutes or until livers are done. Fill cooked crepes with chicken liver mixture; fold over. Place in shallow baking pan. Prepare Hollandaise sauce according to package directions *except* use 1 cup milk. Add green onions, tarragon, and chervil. Spoon over filled crepes. Place under broiler until bubbly. Makes 6 to 8 crepes.

Royal Chicken Crepes

Filled with a delectable creamy sauce and topped with mushrooms.

1 (10 3/4-oz.) can cream of chicken soup,
  not diluted
1 cup dairy sour cream
2 cups cooked chicken or turkey, cubed
1 cup cooked peas (optional)

6 slices dried beef, chopped
12 to 14 warm cooked crepes
1/2 lb. fresh mushrooms, sliced
1/4 cup butter
1/4 teaspoon seasoned salt

In saucepan, combine soup and sour cream; stir in chicken, peas if desired, and dried beef. Heat but do not boil. Fill crepes with hot mixture; fold over. Keep warm. Meanwhile, sauté mushrooms in butter, sprinkle with seasoned salt. Spoon over filled crepes; serve immediately. Makes 12 to 14 crepes.

If peas are added, the mixture will fill 3 or 4 more crepes.

Chicken Saltimbocca Crepes

Perfect for a party! Fill and coat crepes ahead of time and refrigerate. Heat them just before serving.

10 thin slices cooked ham
5 slices mozzarella cheese, halved (about 6-oz.)
10 cooked crepes
1 cup chopped cooked chicken
1 small tomato, finely chopped

Seasoned salt
2 tablespoons grated Parmesan cheese
1/2 cup fine dry bread crumbs
1/4 cup melted butter or margarine

Place one slice of ham and half slice cheese on each crepe. Top with chicken and tomato. Sprinkle with seasoned salt. Fold over right and left sides of crepe and roll up. Combine Parmesan cheese with bread crumbs. Dip rolled crepes in butter, then in bread-crumb mixture. Heat in shallow baking pan at 350°F (177°C) for 20 to 25 minutes. Makes 10 crepes.

Place cooked crepe, brown side down, on board. Arrange slice of ham on each crepe; then cheese, chopped chicken, and tomato.

Fold right and left sides of crepe over filling; then roll up.

Dip rolled-up crepes in shallow dish of melted butter; then into crumbs.

Turkey Enchilada Crepes

A good way to use leftover turkey or inexpensive turkey parts.

1 (4-oz.) can green chiles
2 tablespoons cooking oil
1 clove garlic, minced
1 onion, chopped
4 medium tomatoes, chopped
1 teaspoon salt

1/2 teaspoon dried, crumbled oregano leaves
1/2 cup water
3 cups finely chopped cooked turkey
2 cups dairy sour cream
2 cups grated cheddar cheese
16 to 18 cooked crepes

Drain chiles; rinse seeds away and chop. Heat oil in skillet and sauté chiles with garlic and onion. Stir in tomatoes, salt, oregano, and water. Simmer, uncovered, about 15 minutes or until slightly thickened. Set aside, but keep warm. Meanwhile, combine turkey with sour cream and cheese. Fill cooked crepes with turkey mixture. Roll up; arrange in shallow baking pan. Heat in 350°F (177°C) oven about 20 minutes or until hot and bubbly. Serve with chile-tomato sauce. Makes 16 to 18 enchilada crepes.

Turkey Mushroom Quiche Cups

Try this at your next party—crepe cups filled with turkey quiche.

24 cooked crepes
2 cups finely chopped cooked turkey
2 (2 1/2-oz.) cans sliced mushrooms, drained
1 1/2 cups grated cheddar cheese

1 (10 3/4-oz.) can condensed cream of chicken soup
1/4 cup milk
4 slightly beaten eggs

Line greased muffin pans or custard cups with crepes. Place turkey and mushrooms in each. Sprinkle with cheese. In small saucepan, combine soup and milk. Heat just to boiling, stirring constantly. Gradually stir soup mixture into eggs. Pour soup mixture over cheese. Bake in 350°F (177°C) oven for 20 minutes or until filling is set. Let stand 5 minutes. Serve hot. Makes 24 crepe cups.

Turkey Crepes, Florentine

Magically transforms leftover turkey into a glamorous dish.

1 cup finely diced cooked turkey or chicken
1/2 cup cooked chopped spinach, well drained
1/4 cup cracker crumbs
1/4 cup grated Parmesan cheese
1 tablespoon instant minced onion

1 (10 1/2-oz.) can condensed cream of chicken
  soup
8 to 10 cooked crepes
1/2 cup milk
1/4 cup slivered almonds

Mix turkey, spinach, cracker crumbs, cheese, onion, and *half* the soup. Fill cooked crepes with turkey mixture; roll up. Arrange crepes folded edge down in shallow baking dish. Combine remaining soup with milk. Pour over filled crepes. Sprinkle with almonds. Heat at 350°F (177°C) for 15 to 20 minutes. Makes 8 to 10 crepes.

SEAFOOD

Seafood crepes have always been favorites with famous chefs. Whether you're an experienced chef or a novice homemaker, you'll enjoy true success with these recipes.

There's really nothing mysterious about turning out a spectacular seafood crepe. Start with the basic ingredient—fish or seafood. Usually the fish is fully cooked ahead of time. Then combine it with one of a variety of sauces, including velvety creamy ones, rich cheese flavors, tangy tomato versions, and pungent herb medleys. Fill the cooked crepe with one of these and top with the appropriate topping or garnish to make a savory seafood crepe.

Because there are more varieties of fish and seafood than there are recipes in this book, it is impossible to include recipes to cover each and every kind. I have given suggestions for some of the most popular ones such as shrimp, crab meat, and fish fillets. In most cases, you can substitute one type of fish for another, depending on availability or preference. In fact, many seafood enthusiasts like to combine two or more varieties in one recipe.

At one time fish was an inexpensive dish. With all kinds of fish and seafood increasing in price, everyone is becoming increasingly aware of the cost of a seafood entrée. For those of us who are budget-minded, crepes provide a source of creative dishes without breaking the bank. You can use a minimum amount of fish or seafood and stretch it with a much less costly sauce. The addition of spices and herbs transforms it into a taste delight.

Don't overlook canned fish for great crepes. Canned tuna and salmon are versatile in making crepes. They combine well with eggs, herbs and vegetables to make hearty fare for lunch and dinner. Keep an extra can or two in your pantry so you can use them in crepes on a moment's notice.

Fish has few calories. Crepe batters vary, depending on the amount of butter or oil, flour, milk and eggs. If you're counting calories, use the *Lo-Cal Crepe Batter* or one of the less-rich ones. Watch those sauces and pick one that isn't so calorie-laden. If you're one of those lucky people who doesn't have to be concerned about calories, choose your favorite combinations, cook, and enjoy!

Curried Shrimp Crepes

For all you curry lovers!

3 tablespoons butter or margarine
1/4 cup finely chopped onion
1/4 cup finely chopped celery
1 clove garlic, minced or crushed
1/2 teaspoon curry powder
3 tablespoons flour

1 1/2 cups light cream or milk
1 teaspoon lemon juice
1/2 teaspoon salt
1/8 teaspoon ground ginger
1/2 lb. cooked medium shrimp
10 to 12 warm cooked crepes

In skillet or chafing dish, melt butter. Add onion and celery; sauté until tender. Add garlic, curry powder, and flour; heat until bubbly. Remove from heat and stir in cream, lemon juice, salt, and ginger. Cook on low heat, stirring until thickened. Stir in cooked shrimp. Fill cooked crepes with shrimp mixture; fold over. Serve immediately. Makes 10 to 12 crepes.

Shrimp Marengo

A hearty, spicy shrimp dish!

2 slices bacon, diced
1 onion, chopped
1/2 cup chopped celery
1 clove garlic, minced
1/2 teaspoon salt
1/8 teaspoon pepper
1/4 teaspoon rosemary, crushed

1/4 teaspoon basil
1 (16-oz.) can tomatoes, cut up
1 (6-oz.) can tomato paste
1 lb. uncooked shrimp
1 green pepper, chopped
14 to 16 cooked crepes

Topping:

1 cup sliced fresh mushrooms
2 tablespoons butter

1/4 teaspoon seasoned salt

In large skillet, sauté bacon until done. Remove bacon and set aside. Add onion and celery to bacon drippings. Cook 2 or 3 minutes. Stir in garlic, salt, pepper, rosemary, basil, tomatoes, and tomato paste. Cook uncovered about 10 minutes. Shell shrimp. Add shrimp, green pepper, and cooked bacon to tomato mixture. Simmer several minutes. Fill cooked crepes; fold over. Spoon mushroom topping over. Heat in 350°F (177°C) oven for 10 to 15 minutes. Makes 14 to 16 crepes.

Topping:

In small pan, sauté mushrooms in butter and seasoned salt for several minutes. Spoon over filled crepes.

Lobster Thermidor Crepes

Elegant lobster thermidor wrapped in a delicate crepe!

1 (1 to 1 1/2-lbs.) cooked lobster *or*
   2 (8 to 10-oz.) cooked lobster tails
1/4 cup butter
1/4 cup flour
1 cup light cream or milk
1/4 teaspoon salt
1/8 teaspoon pepper

dash of nutmeg
1/4 cup dry white wine
1/2 cup sliced mushrooms
8 cooked crepes
2 tablespoons melted butter
1/4 cup grated Parmesan cheese

Cut cooked lobster into bite-size pieces; set aside. In saucepan, melt 1/4 cup butter and blend in flour. Stir in cream or milk, salt, pepper, nutmeg, wine, and mushrooms. Cook, stirring constantly, until thickened. Add cooked lobster. Fill cooked crepes with lobster mixture. Fold over; place in broiler pan. Brush crepes with melted butter and top with Parmesan cheese. Broil until golden brown. Serve hot. Makes 8 crepes.

Lobster Newburg Crepes

Enjoy this "Down-East" flavor.

1/4 cup butter or margarine
2 tablespoons flour
1 1/2 cups light cream
3 egg yolks, beaten
1/2 lb. cooked lobster, cut into small
   chunks

1/8 teaspoon paprika
1/4 teaspoon salt
1/8 teaspoon pepper
1/4 cup dry white wine
7 or 8 cooked crepes
Watercress or parsley

In saucepan, melt butter; blend in flour. Add cream. Cook over low heat, stirring constantly until mixture thickens. Stir small amount of hot mixture into egg yolks; then return egg mixture to pan. Cook over low heat, stirring constantly, until thickened. Add lobster, paprika, salt, pepper, and wine. Place crepes in shallow baking pan. Using slotted spoon, fill crepes with lobster mixture; fold over. Pour remaining sauce over all. Heat in 350°F (177°C) oven for 10 to 15 minutes or until hot. Garnish with watercress or parsley. Makes 7 or 8 crepes.

Crab Crepes with Artichoke Hearts

A gourmet favorite.

3 tablespoons butter or margarine
3 tablespoons flour
1 cup milk
1/2 cup chicken bouillon or broth
1/2 cup grated Swiss cheese
2 teaspoons Worcestershire sauce
1 (8-oz.) pkg. frozen artichoke hearts, cooked
   and drained

3 hard-cooked eggs, sliced
1/2 lb. cooked crab meat (fresh, frozen, or
   canned)
12 cooked crepes
1/4 cup grated Parmesan cheese

Melt butter in saucepan. Blend in flour; gradually stir in milk and bouillon. Cook over low heat, stirring constantly, until thickened. Add cheese and Worcestershire sauce. Mix *half* the sauce with artichoke hearts, eggs, and crab meat. Fill crepes with crab mixture; fold over. Place in shallow baking pan. Pour remaining sauce over filled crepes. Sprinkle with Parmesan cheese. Heat in 350°F (177°C) oven for 15 to 20 minutes or until bubbly. Makes 12 crepes.

Deviled Crab Crepes

Luscious rich way to extend crab meat.

1/4 cup chopped onions
1/4 cup butter or margarine
1/4 cup flour
1 tablespoon prepared mustard
1 teaspoon Worcestershire sauce
1/4 teaspoon salt
1 tablespoon chili sauce

1 tablespoon minced parsley
Dash hot pepper sauce
1 1/2 cups milk
1 egg, beaten
1/2 lb. cooked, flaked crab meat
10 to 12 cooked crepes
2 tablespoons melted butter

Cook onions in butter until tender. Stir in flour, mustard, Worcestershire sauce, salt, chili sauce, parsley, and dash of hot pepper sauce. Add milk; cook over low heat, stirring constantly, until thickened. Stir a small amount of hot mixture into beaten egg; then return egg mixture to pan. Cook, stirring for several minutes. Add crab meat. Fill crepes with crab meat mixture; fold over. Brush filled crepes with melted butter. Heat in 350°F (177°C) oven for 10 to 15 minutes. Makes 10 to 12 crepes.

Mandarin Shrimp Crepes

A most impressive dish!

1/2 lb. small uncooked shelled shrimp
2 tablespoons cooking oil
2 tablespoons sliced green onions
1/2 teaspoon ground ginger

1 clove garlic, minced
2 cups Chinese pea pods, fresh or frozen
10 to 12 cooked crepes

Sauce:
2 tablespoons cornstarch
1 tablespoon sugar
1 cup chicken broth or bouillon

1 tablespoon lemon juice
2 tablespoons soy sauce
1 (11-oz.) can mandarin oranges, drained

In large skillet, sauté shrimp in oil for several minutes. Add onions, ginger, garlic, and pea pods. Toss and cook at moderately high heat for 1 or 2 minutes. Fill cooked crepes with shrimp mixture. Roll up or fold over; arrange in shallow baking pan.

Sauce:
In small saucepan, combine cornstarch with sugar; stir in broth, lemon juice, and soy sauce. Cook over low heat, stirring constantly, until thickened and clear. Add drained mandarin oranges. Spoon over filled crepes. Heat in 350°F (177°C) oven for 10 to 15 minutes. Makes 10 to 12 crepes.

Chinese pea pods require very little cooking so add them after shrimp is done; sauté for only a minute or two.

Fill center of cooked crepe with shrimp mixture; fold over and arrange in shallow baking pan before adding sauce.

Crab La Jolla Crepes

Seafarer's delight!

1/4 cup thinly sliced green onions
1/4 cup butter
1/4 cup flour
2 cups light cream
1/2 teaspoon salt
2 teaspoons soy sauce

2 tablespoons dry white wine
2 teaspoons finely chopped canned green chiles
2 cups fresh or frozen crab meat (about 1/2 lb.)
14 warm cooked crepes
1 avocado, thinly sliced

Sauté onions lightly in butter. Blend in flour and cook until bubbly. Stir in cream and salt. Cook, stirring constantly, until thickened. Blend in soy sauce, wine, green chiles, and crab meat. Fill warm crepes with crab mixture; fold over. Garnish with avocado slices. Serve immediately. Makes 14 crepes.

Coquilles St. Jacques (with Crepes)

Famous French scallops recipe made with crepes instead of the usual shell.

1/3 cup dry white wine
2 tablespoons chopped green onion
1/2 lb. scallops, cut into small pieces
1 cup sliced fresh mushrooms
3 tablespoons butter
3 tablespoons flour

1/2 teaspoon salt
1 1/2 cups light cream
2 tablespoons chopped parsley
10 cooked crepes
1/2 cup grated Swiss cheese

In saucepan, combine wine, onion, scallops, and mushrooms. Cover and simmer 5 minutes. Meanwhile, melt butter in skillet. Stir in flour and salt. Pour in light cream; cook, stirring constantly, until thickened. Add parsley; then scallops-mushroom mixture. Fill cooked crepes in shallow baking dish. Fold over. Sprinkle with cheese. Heat in 350°F (177°C) oven for 10 to 15 minutes or until cheese melts. Makes 10 crepes.

Fillet of Sole Crepes

You may substitute perch, haddock, or other fillets available in your market.

1 lb. sole fillets
1/2 teaspoon salt
1/8 teaspoon pepper
2 green onions, sliced
1 lemon, sliced
1/4 cup dry white wine
1 cup fresh mushrooms, sliced

3 tablespoons butter
2 tablespoons flour
1/4 teaspoon paprika
2 egg yolks
1 cup light cream
10 warm cooked crepes

Sprinkle sole with salt and pepper. Place in greased shallow baking pan. Top with onions and lemon slices; pour on wine. Cover and bake at 400°F (205°C) for 15 to 20 minutes or until fish is done. Remove sole; cut into chunks and keep warm. Drain juices that fish was cooked in and set aside. Meanwhile, in skillet, sauté mushrooms in butter. Stir in flour and paprika; cook until bubbly. Gradually add drained juices and cook, stirring until thickened. Beat egg yolks with cream. Stir a little of the hot mixture into eggs. Return egg mixture to pan and cook, stirring constantly, until thickened. Add cooked sole. Fill each cooked crepe with several tablespoons of sole mixture. Fold over. Spoon remaining sauce over. Makes 10 crepes.

Fisherman's Delight Crepes

Yummy cheese sauce covers the fish.

1 lb. fish fillets (haddock, perch, cod, or sole)
1 lemon, sliced
3 tablespoons butter or margarine
3 tablespoons flour
1/2 teaspoon salt
1/8 teaspoon pepper

1/4 teaspoon dry mustard
1/2 teaspoon Worcestershire sauce
1 1/2 cups milk
1 cup grated cheddar cheese
8 to 10 cooked crepes
Paprika

Place fish in skillet with enough boiling water to cover. Add lemon slices. Cover and simmer until fish can be flaked with a fork. Drain and set aside. Melt butter in saucepan; stir in flour, salt, pepper, and mustard. Pour in Worcestershire sauce and milk. Cook over low heat, stirring constantly, until thickened. Add cheese. Cut fish into 1/2-inch pieces. Place crepes in shallow baking pan; fill with cooked fish. Spoon about 1 tablespoon sauce over each; fold over. Pour remaining sauce over all. Sprinkle with paprika. Place under broiler until bubbly. Makes 8 to 10 crepes.

Seafarer's Thermidor

Make your own seafood combination according to availability and family favorites.

1 lb. fish fillets
1 onion slice
1 lemon slice
1 (10 3/4-oz.) can cream of shrimp soup,
    undiluted
3 tablespoons flour
1/4 cup milk
1/4 cup dry white wine

1/2 teaspoon seasoned salt
2 tablespoons finely chopped parsley
1 (4 1/2-oz.) can small shrimp *or* crab meat,
    drained
12 to 14 cooked crepes
1 cup grated mozzarella cheese
1/2 cup soft bread crumbs
1 tablespoon butter or margarine

Place fish in skillet with slices of onion and lemon. Add water to cover fish. Bring to boil; cover and simmer about 5 minutes or until fish is done. Drain; discard onion and lemon slices. Cut fish into bite-size pieces. Meanwhile, in saucepan, blend soup and flour; gradually stir in milk and wine. Cook and stir until thickened and bubbly. Stir in cooked fish, seasoned salt, parsley, and shrimp or crab meat. In large shallow baking pan, fill cooked crepes with seafood. Fold over. Mix cheese with bread crumbs and butter. Sprinkle over filled crepes. Heat in 350°F (177°C) oven for about 15 minutes or until cheese melts. Makes 12 to 14 crepes.

Favorite Tuna Crepes

New dress for a family favorite.

1 (12 1/2-oz.) can tuna, drained
1/2 cup mayonnaise
2 tablespoons instant minced onion
1/2 teaspoon salt
1 (10 3/4-oz.) can condensed cream of celery soup

1/2 cup milk
1 cup grated cheddar cheese
10 cooked crepes

Combine tuna, mayonnaise, onion, and salt; set aside. In small saucepan, mix undiluted soup with milk. Add cheese and heat until cheese is melted. Fill crepes with tuna mixture; roll up and place in shallow baking pan. Pour sauce over crepes. Heat in 350°F (177°C) oven for 20 to 25 minutes. Makes 10 crepes.

Tuna with Herb Sauce

Glamorize tuna this new way.

2 eggs
1 (6 1/2-oz.) can tuna, drained
5 or 6 cooked crepes
1/2 cup mayonnaise
1 teaspoon Dijon mustard
1/4 teaspoon salt

1/8 teaspoon pepper
1 tablespoon sweet pickle relish
1 tablespoon drained capers
1 tablespoon chopped parsley
1/2 teaspoon dried tarragon
1/2 teaspoon dried chervil

Hard cook eggs; peel and cool. Break tuna into small chunks. Fill crepes with tuna. Meanwhile, chop hard-cooked eggs; combine with mayonnaise, mustard, salt, pepper, relish, capers, parsley, tarragon, and chervil. Spoon a small amount of sauce over tuna in crepes. Fold crepes over. Top with remaining sauce. Place under broiler until bubbly. Makes 5 or 6 crepes.

Salmon with Creamed Peas

An interesting fish dish combined with vegetables.

1 (7 3/4-oz.) can salmon
2 hard-cooked eggs, diced
2 tablespoons finely chopped celery
2 green onions, finely chopped
2 tablespoons catsup

2 tablespoons mayonnaise
8 cooked crepes
Melted butter
1 (8-oz.) pkg. frozen peas with cream sauce

Drain and flake salmon. Combine with eggs, celery, onions, catsup, and mayonnaise. Fill crepes; fold over and brush with butter. Place in shallow baking pan. Heat in 350°F (177°C) oven for 10 to 15 minutes. Meanwhile, cook peas according to package directions. Spoon over filled warm crepes. Serve immediately. Makes 8 crepes.

MEATS

The high cost of meat is a common subject for conversation. Everyone complains about it and tries to stretch the meat dollar.

If you have one steak in the refrigerator or freezer and three or four people to feed, let crepes help you stretch that steak into a delicious main dish to satisfy everyone. That's exactly what I do with the *Steak Diane Crepes.*

Thrifty Beef Stroganoff is another budget stretcher. Rather than use the traditional steak for stroganoff, I substitute less expensive round steak. And to help out even more, the meat is extended with a great sauce. The crepe elevates it to company fare at economy rates.

Don't overlook other kinds of meats. Veal is the traditional meat for crepes. It is served in some of the best-known restaurants and most elegant homes. As you know, veal is expensive in most parts of the country so if you like to splurge once in a while without completely wrecking your budget, try one of the veal crepe recipes.

Pork, too, lends itself for use in crepes. It is a natural with sweet-sour type sauces and foods with an oriental flavor.

Leftover meats are great for crepes. Next time you have a pork or beef roast, buy one slightly larger than you need. The next day slice or chop up the leftover meat, combine it with a tasty sauce, and serve it in a crepe.

For a dinner party it's possible to feed a crowd with little or no strain on cook *or* budget using *Party Beef Bourguignon.* The day or night before the party, cook a fairly large boneless roast; cut it into thin slivers and refrigerate with sauce. Also cook crepe batter ahead of time. Just before your guests arrive, fill crepes with meat and wine sauce. Then let dinner heat in the oven while you're greeting guests and enjoying appetizers. You'll impress guests with your culinary ability while you relax and enjoy your own party.

Thrifty Beef Stroganoff Crepes

Round steak substitutes for more expensive steak in this rich-tasting classic dish.

1 1/2 to 2 lbs. round steak, cut into thin strips
1 tablespoon cooking oil
1 onion, chopped
1 teaspoon salt
1/4 teaspoon pepper
1 teaspoon Worcestershire sauce
1 cup beef bouillon or broth

2 tablespoons tomato paste
1 cup sliced fresh mushrooms
2 tablespoons flour
2 tablespoons water
1/4 cup dry red wine
1 cup dairy sour cream
12 warm cooked crepes

In large skillet, brown meat in oil. Add onion, salt, pepper, Worcestershire sauce, bouillon, and tomato paste. Cover and cook over moderate heat for about 35 to 45 minutes or until meat is tender. Stir in mushrooms. Dissolve flour in water; add to meat mixture. Cook, stirring over moderate heat until thickened and bubbly. Stir in wine, then sour cream. Heat, but do not boil. Fill warm crepes with meat and sauce; fold over. Serve immediately. Makes 12 crepes.

Small pieces of meat fit into crepes better than thick chunks, so cut round steak into thin strips for this Stroganoff.

Gently stir in sour cream after meat is done and mixture is thickened. Then heat the Stroganoff, but do not boil.

Steak Diane Crepes

Super way to stretch a steak!

3 tablespoons butter or margarine
1 lb. beef fillet or top sirloin, cut into thin
    strips
1/4 teaspoon salt
1/8 teaspoon pepper
1 teaspoon lemon juice

2 teaspoons Worcestershire sauce
1 teaspoon Dijon mustard
2 tablespoons chopped chives
1 tablespoon chopped parsley
8 warm crepes

Melt butter in skillet; add meat and brown quickly. Stir in salt, pepper, lemon juice, Worcestershire sauce, mustard, chives, and parsley. Heat to boiling. Fill warm crepes with meat and juices. Fold over. Serve immediately. Makes 8 crepes

Deviled Steak Crepes

Spicy round steak dressed up in a crepe.

1 to 1 1/2 lbs. beef round steak
1/4 cup flour
1 small onion, chopped
1 clove garlic, minced
3 tablespoons cooking oil
1/2 cup water
1 (8-oz.) can tomato sauce

2 tablespoons vinegar
2 teaspoons horseradish
2 teaspoons prepared mustard
1/2 teaspoon salt
1/4 teaspoon pepper
10 to 12 warm cooked crepes

Cut meat into thin strips; coat with flour. In skillet, brown meat, onion, and garlic in hot oil. Stir in water, tomato sauce, vinegar, horseradish, mustard, salt, and pepper. Cover and simmer for 45 to 50 minutes or until meat is tender. Fill warm crepes with meat mixture; fold over and serve immediately. Makes 10 to 12 crepes.

Quick Hamburger Stroganoff Crepes

A family favorite, dressed up in crepes.

1 small onion, chopped
1 tablespoon cooking oil
1 lb. lean ground beef
1 (10 1/2-oz.) can cream of mushroom soup, undiluted
1/2 teaspoon salt

2 tablespoons catsup
1 (2-oz.) can sliced mushrooms, drained
1/2 cup dairy sour cream
12 cooked crepes
2 tablespoons melted butter

In skillet, sauté onion in oil; add beef and cook several minutes. Pour off excess fat. Stir in undiluted soup, salt, catsup, and mushrooms. Heat to boiling. Remove from heat; stir in sour cream. In shallow baking pan, fill cooked crepes with meat mixture. Fold over. Brush with butter. Heat in 350°F (177°C) oven for 10 to 15 minutes. Makes 12 crepes.

Swedish Meatballs

A new and different way to serve meatballs.

1 lb. lean ground beef
1 egg, slightly beaten
1/3 cup milk
1/2 cup soft bread crumbs
1 teaspoon salt
1/8 teaspoon ground mace
1/8 teaspoon pepper
1/4 cup minced onion

1 tablespoon cooking oil
2 tablespoons flour
1 bouillon cube, crumbled
1/2 cup milk
1 cup dairy sour cream
1 teaspoon dried dill weed
1/2 teaspoon seasoned salt
8 to 10 warm cooked crepes

Combine beef with egg, milk, bread crumbs, salt, mace, pepper, and onion. Shape into meatballs about 1 inch in diameter. Heat oil in large skillet; add meatballs. Cook over moderate heat, turning several times. Remove meatballs as they get done; keep warm. Stir flour and crumbled bouillon cube into meat juices. Add milk, stirring until thickened. Stir in sour cream, dill, and seasoned salt; heat but do not boil. Arrange 3 meatballs in center of each crepe; fold over. Spoon sour cream sauce over filled crepes. Serve hot. Makes 8 to 10 crepes.

Old English Beef Crepes

A glamorous dish with thin slices of roast beef or pot roast.

2 small onions, thinly sliced
2 tablespoons butter or margarine
1/4 teaspoon seasoned salt
1/2 lb. cooked roast beef, thinly sliced
6 to 8 cooked crepes

1 cup dairy sour cream
1 tablespoon horseradish
1/4 teaspoon salt
Dash of paprika

In skillet, cook onions in butter several minutes; sprinkle with seasoned salt. Arrange on crepes with roast beef. Fold crepes over. Place in shallow baking pan; cover with foil. Heat in 350°F (177°C) oven about 10 minutes or until warm. Meanwhile, combine sour cream with horseradish, salt, and paprika. Spoon over filled crepes. Makes 6 to 8 crepes.

Party Beef Bourguignon

An easy way to prepare this popular dish for a party. If convenient, cook meat the day before; then fill crepes just before guests arrive and heat at serving time.

1 (3 to 3 1/2 lbs.) boneless pot roast
Salt and pepper
1 pkg. dry onion soup mix
1 (10 1/2-oz.) can condensed cream of
    mushroom soup

1 cup dry red wine
1 cup water
1/3 cup flour
1 (4-oz.) can sliced mushrooms, drained
22 to 25 cooked crepes

Sprinkle meat with salt and pepper. Place in large pot or Dutch oven. Add dry onion soup mix, mushroom soup (not diluted), wine, and 1 cup water. Cover and simmer 3 to 4 hours or until meat is tender. Remove beef. Dissolve flour in small amount of water. Stir into juices left in pot. Cook over low heat until thickened, stirring constantly. Stir in mushrooms. Meanwhile, slice beef into small slivers about 1/2 inch thick and 2 inches long. Place 3 or 4 tablespoons beef slices in center of each cooked crepe in large shallow baking pan. Spoon about 1 tablespoon sauce over each. Fold crepes over. Pour remaining sauce over filled crepes. Cover and heat in 350°F (177°C) oven for 15 to 20 minutes or until hot. Makes 22 to 25 crepes.

Hungarian Veal with Mushrooms

Superb dining!

2 tablespoons cooking oil
1 onion, chopped
1 tablespoon chopped parsley
1 teaspoon salt
1 teaspoon paprika
1/8 teaspoon pepper

1 lb. veal cutlets, cut into thin strips
1/2 lb. fresh mushrooms, thinly sliced
1 cup dairy sour cream
12 warm cooked crepes
Sour cream for garnish (optional)

Heat oil in skillet. Add onion and cook several minutes. Stir in parsley, salt, paprika, pepper, and veal. Cover and cook several minutes or until meat is tender. Add mushrooms; cook until tender. Stir in sour cream. Fill cooked crepes; fold over. Garnish with extra sour cream, if desired. Serve immediately. Makes 12 crepes.

Swiss Veal

Here's an elegant dish in a hurry.

3 tablespoons butter
3/4 lb. veal cutlets, cut into thin strips
2 tablespoons chopped green onion
1/2 cup sliced mushrooms
1/2 teaspoon salt
1/8 teaspoon pepper

1 tablespoon flour
1/2 cup light cream
1/4 cup dry white wine
8 warm cooked crepes
Minced parsley

In skillet, melt butter. Add veal, onion, and mushrooms; sauté until lightly browned. Stir in salt, pepper, and flour. Add cream; cook, stirring, until mixture boils. Pour in wine. Fill crepes; fold over. Sprinkle with parsley. Serve immediately. Makes 8 crepes.

Veal Oscar Crepes

Elegant and delicious dining—one of the very best!

1 lb. veal cutlets
2 tablespoons butter
1/2 teaspoon salt
1/8 teaspoon pepper

1 lb. fresh or frozen asparagus
8 warm cooked crepes
8 crab legs

Bearnaise Sauce:
1 teaspoon chopped shallots *or* chives
3 tablespoons white wine
1/2 teaspoon dried tarragon
1/2 cup butter

3 egg yolks
1/8 teaspoon salt
1 tablespoon chopped parsley
1 teaspoon lemon juice

Cut veal into thin strips. In skillet, sauté meat in hot butter. Add salt and pepper. Meanwhile cook asparagus; drain. Fill cooked crepes with asparagus and veal. Top with crab meat. Fold crepes over. Top with bearnaise sauce. Serve immediately. Makes 8 crepes.

Bearnaise Sauce:
Combine shallots, wine, and tarragon in saucepan. Cook at moderately high heat about 5 minutes. Cool slightly. Heat butter until bubbly. Pour wine mixture into blender. Add egg yolks and salt; turn blender on and off quickly to blend ingredients. Turn on; gradually pour bubbling hot butter through center hole of blender top. Stir in parsley and lemon juice.

Chinese Pork Rolls

All the good ingredients of famous Chinese dishes—wrapped in crepes.

1 small Chinese cabbage, finely sliced
1 (6-oz.) can water chestnuts, chopped
1/3 cup chopped green onions
3 cups boiling water
1/4 teaspoon salt
2 tablespoons soy sauce
1/4 cup catsup

1 tablespoon lemon juice
1 tablespoon honey
2 cups finely chopped cooked pork
36 cooked crepes
1 egg, beaten
Cooking oil

In large mixing bowl, combine cabbage with water chestnuts and green onions. Pour boiling water over them. Let stand 5 minutes. Drain thoroughly. Stir in salt, soy sauce, catsup, lemon juice, honey, and pork. Place about 2 tablespoons of the mixture on each cooked crepe. Fold bottom of crepe over the filling; then fold in both sides and finally the top. Brush overlapping edges with beaten egg; press together to hold in filling. Carefully drop filled crepes into at least 1 1/2 inches of hot oil in skillet or deep fryer at 350°F (177°C). Fry until brown. Serve hot with sweet-sour sauce or hot Chinese mustard. Makes 36 pork rolls.

Sweet and Sour Pork Crepes

Glamorous way to dress up leftover pork roast.

1 tablespoon cooking oil
2 cups cooked lean pork, cut into strips
1 small green pepper, cut into strips
1 (8-oz.) can sliced pineapple, not drained
1 cup chicken bouillon
2 tablespoons soy sauce
1/4 cup vinegar

1/4 cup sugar
1 tablespoon cornstarch
2 tablespoons cold water
1 (8-oz.) can water chestnuts, sliced
12 cooked crepes
2 tablespoons melted butter
2 tablespoons sesame seeds, toasted

In large skillet, heat oil; lightly brown pork. Stir in green pepper. Cut pineapple into chunks; add pineapple with juice, bouillon, soy sauce, vinegar, and sugar. Dissolve cornstarch in water. Stir into hot mixture. Cook on low heat, stirring constantly until thickened. Stir in water chestnuts. In large shallow pan, spoon several tablespoons pork mixture in center of each crepe. Fold over. Brush with butter, then sprinkle with sesame seeds. Heat in 350°F (177°C) oven for 10 to 15 minutes. Makes 12 crepes.

FOREIGN INTRIGUE

The crepe is international! People throughout the world have enjoyed them for centuries; each country has its own version and name. Here in North America, our food customs have a rich heritage borrowed from many other lands. Our forefathers brought a variety of styles of cooking with them. In many homes, ethnic styles of cooking have been handed down from one generation to another.

To modernize these international favorites, I use ingredients and flavors similar to the Old World specialties. However, my recipes use equipment, techniques and foods available in our local stores. For example, all the crepe batters can be used with either the traditional crepe pans or the new upside-down crepe griddles. And, even though the sauce ideas were borrowed from world-wide cuisines, we can relate to them because we are used to seeing and eating them in other forms.

In Mexico the tortilla is used as a shell or edible container to hold foods. Most of us have tasted the tortilla converted into an enchilada, taco or burrito. Crepes combine well with the ingredients used in these Mexican-type dishes. In general, the results are lighter and more delicate than dishes made with the original ingredients.

Variations of Italian favorite recipes are also given. Instead of the usual pasta and rice, the crepe provides a pleasant variation. Italian sauces, whether tomato or cheese, make a savory combination with crepes.

It's fun to experience the varied tastes and techniques of cuisines around the world. Even though the homemaker in Hong Kong may not make Sweet-Sour Chicken the same way we do and a chef in Rome would not approve of some of our prepared sauces, these recipes are adapted to our way of life. Some of the recipes are made from scratch while others use packaged or canned sauces available in our markets.

If you have an ethnic favorite, use these recipes as a guide to convert your favorite flavor into an unusual crepe dish.

Manicotti Crepes

A hearty main dish that extends the meat.

1 (10-oz.) pkg. frozen chopped spinach
1 onion, chopped
1 clove garlic, minced
2 tablespoons butter
1 lb. ground beef
1/2 teaspoon salt

1/8 teaspoon pepper
1/4 cup grated Parmesan cheese
12 cooked crepes
1 (8-oz.) pkg. mozzarella cheese cut into thin
  slices

Sauce:
1/4 cup butter
1/4 cup flour
2 1/2 cups milk

1/2 teaspoon salt
1/8 teaspoon pepper
1/4 cup grated Parmesan cheese

Cook spinach according to package directions. Drain well. In large skillet, sauté onion and garlic in butter until golden brown. Add beef and brown, stirring frequently. Remove from heat. Pour off excess grease. Stir in spinach, salt, pepper, and Parmesan cheese. Fill crepes with mixture and roll up loosely. Place in large shallow baking pan; top crepes with mozzarella cheese slices.

To make sauce:
Melt butter in saucepan; blend in flour and gradually stir in milk. Cook and stir until sauce thickens and comes to a boil. Stir in salt, pepper, and Parmesan cheese.

Spoon sauce over cheese slices and crepes. Bake at 350°F (177°C) for 20 minutes or until bubbly. Makes 12 crepes.

Italian Mushroom Crepes

Delightful combination of mushrooms with salami and cheese.

12 fresh mushrooms, finely chopped
1/4 cup finely chopped green onion
2 tablespoons butter
1/2 cup finely diced salami

1/2 cup finely diced Monterey Jack cheese
6 to 8 cooked crepes
2 tablespoons melted butter

In small skillet, sauté mushrooms with onions in 2 tablespoons butter. Remove from heat. Add salami and cheese. Spoon about 3 tablespoons onto center of each cooked crepe. Roll up. Place in a shallow baking pan. Brush with 2 tablespoons melted butter. Heat in 350°F (177°C) oven for 15 minutes. Makes 6 to 8 crepes.

Italiano Spinach Cups

Similar to a quiche—with an Italian accent.

1 (10-oz.) pkg. frozen chopped spinach
1 cup ricotta cheese
1/2 cup grated Parmesan cheese
1 tablespoon instant minced onion
1/2 teaspoon oregano

1/4 teaspoon salt
1 egg, beaten slightly
10 cooked crepes
1/2 cup finely chopped pepperoni
Dairy sour cream (optional)

Thaw spinach; *squeeze dry*. Mix with ricotta, Parmesan, onion, oregano, salt, and egg. Line greased muffin pans or custard cups with cooked crepes. Sprinkle pepperoni in bottom of each. Spoon about 3 tablespoons cheese-spinach mixture into each crepe cup. Bake at 350°F (177°C) for about 15 minutes or until a light golden color on top. Cool several minutes; remove from pan. Garnish tops with sour cream if desired. Makes 10 spinach cups.

Cheese Blintzes

Once an ethnic dish, its popularity has now spread far beyond the traditional Jewish kitchen to homes everywhere.

2 cups small-curd cottage cheese
1 egg yolk
2 tablespoons sugar
1 tablespoon lemon juice
12 to 14 cooked crepes

2 tablespoons butter
Powdered sugar
Dairy sour cream
Preserves

Drain cottage cheese in strainer or colander for at least 1/2 hour; then gently press out any excess liquid with back of spoon. In a bowl mix cottage cheese with egg yolk, sugar, and lemon juice. Spoon filling onto center of cooked crepes. Fold over bottom, both sides, and top. Melt butter in skillet; lightly brown blintzes on both sides. Sprinkle with powdered sugar. Serve warm with sour cream and your favorite preserves. Makes 12 to 14 blintzes.

Cannelloni Style Crepes

Crepes with Italian influence.

1 cup small-curd cottage cheese
1 (3-oz.) pkg. cream cheese, softened
2 tablespoons butter, softened
2 tablespoons chopped parsley
1 egg, beaten

1 tablespoon chopped green onion
1/8 teaspoon salt
8 cooked crepes
1 (15-oz.) can Italian-style Marinara Sauce
1/4 cup grated Parmesan cheese

In medium mixing bowl, combine cottage cheese, cream cheese, butter, parsley, egg, green onion, and salt. Spoon 3 tablespoons of cheese mixture into center of each cooked crepe. Roll up; place in shallow baking pan. Pour Marinara Sauce over filled crepes; sprinkle with Parmesan cheese. Bake in 350°F (177°C) oven for 20 to 30 minutes. Makes 8 crepes.

Cheese Blintzes II

Popular blintzes made with dry cottage cheese filling.

1 lb. dry cottage cheese
1 (3-oz.) pkg. cream cheese, softened
2 tablespoons soft butter
1/2 teaspoon vanilla
1/4 cup sugar

20 cooked crepes
1/4 cup butter
2 tablespoons cooking oil
Dairy sour cream
Sweetened fresh fruit *or* apricot preserves

In small mixer bowl, combine cottage cheese, cream cheese, 2 tablespoons butter, vanilla, and sugar. Mix thoroughly. Spread about 2 tablespoons cheese filling in center of each crepe. Fold over bottom, both sides, and top. Heat 1/4 cup butter and oil in large skillet. Lightly brown blintzes on both sides. Serve warm with sour cream and fruit or preserves. Makes about 20 blintzes.

Burrito Crepes

For a modern version of a burrito, try this recipe with Cornmeal or All-Purpose Crepes.

8 cooked crepes
1 (17-oz.) can refried beans
1 cup grated cheddar cheese

1/4 cup finely chopped green chiles
1 cup grated cheddar cheese

Sauce:
1 (7-oz.) can green chile salsa
1 medium tomato, finely chopped

1 small onion, finely chopped

Spread cooked crepes with refried beans; sprinkle with 1 cup cheese and chiles. Shape into Burrito Roll and place folded edge down in lightly greased shallow 9" x 13" baking dish. Sprinkle all with remaining 1 cup cheese. Heat in 350°F (177°C) oven for 10 to 15 minutes or until cheese melts. Serve with sauce made of chile salsa combined with tomato and onion. Makes 8 crepes.

Chili Cheese Stack

A new variation of ever-popular chili.

1 lb. ground beef
1/4 cup chopped green pepper
1/4 cup chopped onion
2 (8-oz.) cans tomato sauce
1 (15-oz.) can kidney beans, drained

1 teaspoon chili powder
1/2 teaspoon salt
Dash hot pepper sauce
8 cooked crepes
2 cups shredded Monterey Jack cheese

Brown meat in skillet. Drain off excess grease; stir in green pepper and onion. Cook until tender. Add tomato sauce, kidney beans, chili powder, salt, and hot pepper sauce. Bring to boil; simmer several minutes. In 9-inch pie plate or shallow casserole, stack layers of cooked crepes filled with meat mixture. Sprinkle small amount of cheese on each layer, saving about half of the cheese for the top. Heat in 350°F (177°C) oven for 10 to 15 minutes or until cheese melts. Cut stack into 5 or 6 wedges.

Beef & Bean Burritos

If you like burritos, this variation with crepes will become your favorite.

1 (14-oz.) can refried beans
12 cooked crepes
2 cups cooked beef, finely chopped
1 1/2 cups diced Jack cheese

Hot pepper sauce (optional)
1 avocado, thinly sliced
1 (7-oz.) can green chile salsa

Spread about 2 tablespoons beans along center of each crepe. Combine beef and cheese; spoon about 1/4 cup on top of beans. Sprinkle with hot pepper sauce, if desired. Top with several thin slices of avocado. Fold bottom and top, roll up and place in shallow baking pan. Cover and heat in 350°F (177°C) oven for 15 to 20 minutes. Serve with green chile salsa. Makes 12 burritos.

Crepe Tostadas

Although crepes aren't as crispy as tortillas for tostadas, they're quite tasty. Especially good with Cornmeal Crepes.

8 cooked crepes
1 (17-oz.) can refried beans
1 lb. lean ground beef
1 (1 1/4-oz.) pkg. taco seasoning mix
1 cup water
1 1/2 cups grated cheddar cheese

2 cups shredded lettuce
1 large tomato, chopped
1 avocado, peeled and sliced
1/2 cup dairy sour cream (optional)
Taco sauce or Russian dressing

Place a single layer of cooked crepes on cookie sheet in 400°F (205°C) oven. Heat about 5 minutes or until crispy around edges. Keep warm while making filling. Heat refried beans in saucepan. Meanwhile, brown beef in large skillet; pour off excess grease. Stir in dry taco mix and water. Stir and bring to boil. Reduce heat; simmer, uncovered, 15 to 20 minutes, stirring occasionally. Spread hot beans on crepes; then a layer of meat mixture. Top with cheese, lettuce, and chopped tomato. Garnish with avocado and sour cream, if desired. Serve with taco sauce or Russian dressing. Makes 8 Crepe Tostadas.

Swiss Enchiladas

Eye-appealing crepes with red filling and yellow topping. Garnish with ripe olives for a finishing touch.

1 onion, chopped
1 tablespoon cooking oil
1 clove garlic, minced
1 (15-oz.) can tomato purée
2 canned green chiles, seeded and chopped
2 cups chopped cooked chicken

1/2 teaspoon salt
10 to 12 cooked crepes
1/2 lb. grated Jack or American cheese
3 chicken bouillon cubes, crumbled
1 cup light cream

In large saucepan, sauté onion in oil until soft. Add garlic, tomato purée, chiles, chicken, and salt. Simmer about 10 minutes. In large shallow baking pan, spoon tomato-chicken mixture onto center of each cooked crepe. Fold over. Combine cheese with bouillon cubes and cream. Pour over filled crepes. Bake at 350°F (177°C) for 20 to 25 minutes. Serve hot. Makes 10 to 12 crepes.

Old Tavern Crepes

Men really go for this one!

3 tablespoons butter
1 small onion, finely chopped
1 cup sliced mushrooms
3/4 cup beer
1/4 cup light cream
1/2 cup cooked ham, cut into thin strips
1 tablespoon cornstarch

2 tablespoons cold water
1/2 teaspoon salt
1/8 teaspoon pepper
1 cup grated Swiss cheese
10 cooked crepes
1 cup grated Swiss cheese

In skillet, melt butter; add onion and mushrooms. Cook over medium heat several minutes. Stir in beer, then cream and ham. Simmer 2 or 3 minutes. Dissolve cornstarch in 2 tablespoons cold water. Add to mushroom mixture. Season with salt and pepper. Cook on low heat until mixture thickens. Stir in 1 cup grated cheese. Fill cooked crepes; fold over. Place in shallow baking pan. Sprinkle with remaining cup of cheese. Broil until cheese melts. Makes 10 crepes.

Swiss Enchilada Crepes

Chinese Egg Rolls

A great imitation of Chinese egg rolls.

1 cup chopped cooked chicken
1 (16-oz.) can Chinese vegetables, drained
1/4 cup minced green onions
1/2 teaspoon ground ginger
1/4 cup ground almonds

2 teaspoons soy sauce
1 teaspoon sugar
1/4 teaspoon almond extract
14 to 16 warm cooked crepes
Hot oil for deep frying

Mix chicken with Chinese vegetables, onions, ginger, almonds, soy sauce, sugar, and almond extract. Place about 2 tablespoons mixture on each crepe; fold over sides and roll up. Seal edges with a little batter left from making crepes or with slightly beaten egg. Drop each into pan of hot oil (350°F/177°C) and fry until golden color. Drain. Cut into smaller pieces, if desired. Serve hot. Makes 14 to 16 egg rolls.

Polynesian Crepes

Reminiscent of the South Seas!

2 tablespoons butter or margarine
1 medium onion, sliced
1 green pepper, cut into small chunks
1 (8-oz.) can pineapple chunks, not drained
1 tablespoon vinegar
1 tablespoon honey

1 tablespoon soy sauce
2 tablespoons cornstarch
1 cup chicken bouillon
2 cups cooked ham, cut into small chunks
14 to 16 warm cooked crepes
1/3 cup chopped macadamia nuts *or* cashews

Melt butter in large skillet; stir in onion and green pepper. Cook over moderate heat for several minutes. Add pineapple, vinegar, honey, and soy sauce. Dissolve cornstarch in bouillon. Add to hot mixture and cook, stirring until thickened. Stir in ham and heat. Fill warm crepes; fold over. Sprinkle with nuts; serve immediately. Makes 14 to 16 crepes.

Sweet-Sour Chicken

Compares with the best dishes in fine Chinese restaurants. Equally good when made with turkey.

2 whole chicken breasts, boned and cut into slivers
2 tablespoons cooking oil
1 carrot, thinly sliced
1 cup sliced mushrooms
1 small green pepper, cut into slivers
4 green onions, sliced
1 cup chicken broth or bouillon

1 tablespoon vinegar
1 tablespoon brown sugar
1/2 teaspoon salt
2 tablespoons cornstarch
2 tablespoons soy sauce
1 tomato, chopped
12 warm cooked crepes
2 tablespoons toasted sesame seeds

In skillet, heat oil; stir in chicken and carrot. Stir-fry for several minutes. Add mushrooms, green pepper, and green onions. Cook for 1 minute. Pour in broth or bouillon, vinegar, sugar, and salt. Dissolve cornstarch in soy sauce. Add to mixture. Stir in tomato. Cover pan; cook on low heat several minutes or until done. Fill warm crepes with mixture; fold over. Top with sesame seeds. Serve immediately. Makes 12 crepes.

Taco Crepes

Thinner than a regular taco, with the same flavors and shape.

8 to 10 cooked crepes
Foil
1 pound lean ground beef
1 (1 1/4-oz.) pkg. taco seasoning mix
1 cup water

1 1/2 cups grated cheddar cheese
2 cups shredded lettuce
2 small tomatoes, chopped
Taco sauce (optional)

For a crispy taco, place cooked crepes on cookie sheet. Fold each crepe in half with crumpled foil inside to hold it open for filling. Heat in 325°F (163°C) oven with crumpled foil inside crepes for about 10 to 12 minutes or until crisp. Meanwhile, brown ground beef, stirring until crumbly. Drain off excess fat. Stir in seasoning mix and water. Bring to boil. Simmer uncovered, 15 to 20 minutes, stirring occasionally. Spoon into crisp crepe-taco shells. Place cheese, lettuce, and tomatoes on top. Serve with taco sauce if desired. Makes 8 to 10 taco crepes.

Bombay Curried Eggs

A new slant for egg lovers—curry with all the trimmings!

1/4 cup butter or margarine
1 teaspoon curry powder
1/8 teaspoon ground ginger
1/4 teaspoon salt
1/8 teaspoon garlic salt
1 tablespoon instant minced onion
1/8 teaspoon grated lemon peel
1/2 cup raisins
1 small tart apple; peeled, cored, and finely
   chopped

3 tablespoons flour
1 cup chicken broth or bouillon
1 cup light cream
5 hard-cooked eggs, peeled and diced
4 slices bacon, cooked and crumbled
12 to 14 warm cooked crepes
1/4 cup coconut

Melt butter with curry powder, ginger, salt, garlic salt, and onion. Add lemon peel, raisins and apple; cook several minutes. Blend in flour. Then slowly pour in broth and cream. Simmer, stirring, until bubbly and thick. Stir in eggs and bacon. Fill warm cooked crepes with eggs and sauce; fold over. Sprinkle tops with coconut. Serve hot. Makes 12 to 14 crepes. Serve with chutney.

In skillet, add grated lemon peel, raisins, and chopped apple to melted butter and spices.

After sauce is thickened, stir chopped eggs and crumbled bacon into curry mixture.

Spoon finished curry along center of warm crepes; fold over and sprinkle with coconut.

CHEESE & EGG

The happy union of cheese and eggs has probably created more delicious crepes than any other combination of foods. These two versatile foods form the basis of an unending number of crepe variations.

They are perfect for breakfast or brunch. You can use them in all kinds of crepe recipes from scrambled eggs with cheese to the more elegant *Eggs Continental*.

One of my favorites is the *Quiche Lorraine Crepe*. It can be served anytime, but it seems especially appropriate for a Sunday brunch. Those little cups, shaped like flower petals and filled with a delectable egg and cheese combination create a happy atmosphere. Vary the flavor by substituting chopped ham, mushrooms or shrimp. In forming the cups, choose the smallest crepes to fit into the muffin pans and make sure there are no holes in them, so the mixture doesn't leak out. If you like these cups, you can fill them with almost any entrée mixture that requires a short baking time.

Many egg dishes are adaptable to crepes. Perhaps Eggs Benedict is the star performer. It has the reputation of a difficult-to-make sophisticated dish, but that isn't really true. If you make *Eggs Benedict Crepes* for your guests, you'll be known as an avant-garde cook. When preparing this dish, I found the egg fits more gracefully into the crepe if the crepe is folded in half rather than the traditional fold.

So many kinds of cheese are used in crepes that I hardly know which to select as my favorites. The most frequent sauce-maker is cheddar cheese. It combines well with most other foods and makes a great topping on filled crepes. Then, there's the good old stand-by, Parmesan. It tastes so great and smells so good while being broiled that it's a temptation to top almost all the entrée crepes with it. Probably next in popularity are Swiss and Monterey Jack cheeses. Swiss is used for Quiche as well as some of the creamy sauces over seafood and vegetables. Jack cheese is perfect for almost all Mexican-type dishes. If you don't have the kind of cheese suggested in the recipe, try another variety—the taste will be different, but still delicious.

Brunch Egg Cups

For that special brunch.

6 cooked crepes

1 (3-oz.) can sliced mushrooms

6 eggs

Salt and pepper

6 tablespoons light cream

1/2 cup grated Swiss cheese

Brush muffin pans or custard cups with butter. Line each with a cooked crepe. Place several mushroom slices in each. Break one egg in each cup. Sprinkle with salt and pepper. Spoon 1 tablespoon cream over each egg; sprinkle with cheese. Bake at 325°F (163°C) for 20 to 30 minutes or until eggs are set. Makes 6 egg cups.

Eggs Benedict Crepes

A delicious breakfast or brunch favorite in crepe form.

6 to 8 eggs

6 to 8 slices Canadian bacon or cooked ham

6 to 8 warm cooked crepes

Sauce:

4 egg yolks

1/4 teaspoon salt

1/2 teaspoon dry mustard

1 tablespoon lemon juice

1/4 lb. butter (1 stick)

Sliced ripe olives (optional)

Paprika (optional)

Poach eggs to desired degree of doneness. Lightly sauté bacon or ham. Place slice of bacon or ham on lower half of each cooked crepe. Top ham with poached egg. Then fold top half of crepe over ham and egg. Spoon sauce over all. Garnish with sliced ripe olives and paprika, if desired. Serve hot. Makes 6 to 8 crepes.

Sauce:

Put egg yolks, salt, mustard, and lemon juice in blender. Cover and blend on low until eggs are well mixed. Heat butter until melted and bubbly hot. Immediately pour butter in steady stream through the small hole in top of blender, keeping blender on low until mixture is thickened. Keep warm in bowl over hot, not boiling, water.

Huevos Rancheros Crepes

A new variation of the old Mexican favorite.

2 slices bacon, diced
2 tablespoons minced onion
1 (4-oz.) can chopped green chiles
1 (14 1/2-oz.) can tomatoes, cut up

8 eggs
1/4 teaspoon salt
8 warm cooked crepes

In large skillet, fry bacon until crisp. Remove bacon and set aside. Add onion, chiles, and tomatoes to bacon drippings. Simmer about 5 minutes. Break eggs into tomato mixture. Sprinkle with salt. Cover and cook until eggs are desired degree of doneness. With spatula, place one cooked egg on center of each cooked crepe; spoon about 1 tablespoon of sauce over egg. Fold over. Add cooked bacon to remaining sauce. Pour over filled crepes. Serve immediately. Makes 8 crepes.

Surprise Eggs

Sunday morning surprise!

5 eggs
1/4 cup milk
1/4 teaspoon salt
1 tablespoon butter
1/2 cup Monterey Jack cheese, cut into small cubes

2 tablespoons finely chopped canned green chiles
5 or 6 warm cooked crepes
1/3 cup dairy sour cream
1 avocado, peeled and sliced

Mix eggs with milk and salt. Melt butter in skillet. Pour in egg mixture. Stir gently and cook over medium heat. When almost set, stir in cheese and chili peppers. Cook to desired degree of doneness. Fill warm crepes; fold over. Top with sour cream. Garnish with avocado slices. Serve immediately. Makes 5 or 6 crepes.

Quiche Lorraine Cups

A new version of the traditional gourmet recipe.

12 cooked crepes
4 slices bacon
1 cup grated Swiss cheese
2 tablespoons flour

1/4 teaspoon salt
2 eggs, beaten
1 cup milk

Line greased muffin pans or custard cups with cooked crepes. Cook bacon until crisp; drain and crumble. Sprinkle in crepe shells. Top with cheese. Mix flour, salt, and eggs with milk; pour over cheese. Bake in 350°F (177°C) oven for 15 to 20 minutes or until firm. Cool 5 minutes before removing from pan. Serve hot. Makes 12 crepe cups.

After lining muffin pans with cooked crepes, spoon grated cheese and crumbled bacon into bottom.

Combine milk-and-egg mixture in large measuring cup for easy pouring into crepe cups.

Farmer's Brunch Crepes

For a hearty and filling brunch.

4 hard-cooked eggs, peeled and sliced
1 cup diced cooked ham
1 medium potato, cooked, peeled, and chopped
1/2 teaspoon salt
18 to 20 cooked crepes
2 tablespoons butter

2 tablespoons flour
1/2 teaspoon salt
1/8 teaspoon pepper
1 cup chicken bouillon
1 cup dairy sour cream

In mixing bowl, combine hard-cooked eggs with ham, potato, and 1/2 teaspoon salt. Fill cooked crepes with egg mixture; roll or fold over. Place in shallow baking pan. Melt butter in small sauce-pan. Stir in flour and cook until bubbly. Add 1/2 teaspoon salt, pepper, and bouillon. Cook, stirring constantly, until thick and smooth. Remove from heat. Gradually stir sauce into sour cream. Spoon over filled crepes. Heat in 350°F (177°C) oven for 10 to 15 minutes or until hot. Makes 18 to 20 crepes.

Eggs Continental

Perfect brunch or Sunday night supper.

4 hard-cooked eggs, sliced
8 cooked crepes
3 slices bacon, diced and cooked
1 cup dairy sour cream
1 tablespoon milk
1 teaspoon instant minced onion

1/2 teaspoon salt
1/4 teaspoon paprika
1/8 teaspoon pepper
1 cup grated cheddar cheese
1/4 cup dry bread crumbs
1 tablespoon melted butter or margarine

Arrange eggs over center of cooked crepes, allowing 1/2 egg to each crepe. Combine bacon with sour cream, milk, onion, salt, paprika, and pepper. Spoon over eggs. Fold over; arrange in shallow baking pan. Cover top with cheese. Toss bread crumbs with butter; sprinkle over cheese. Heat in 350°F (177°C) oven for 10 to 15 minutes. Makes 8 crepes.

Dairyland Scrambled Egg Crepes

Cottage cheese adds protein to this nutritious dish.

2 tablespoons butter
6 eggs, beaten slightly
1/2 cup cottage cheese
1/2 teaspoon salt
1/8 teaspoon pepper

1 teaspoon dried dill weed
10 to 12 warm cooked crepes
2 tablespoons minced parsley or chives
Dairy sour cream (optional)

Melt butter in skillet. Pour in eggs; then stir in cottage cheese, salt, and pepper. Cook, stirring constantly, until set but moist. Add dill weed. Fill warm cooked crepes with eggs; roll up. Sprinkle with parsley or chives. Top with dairy sour cream, if desired. Serve immediately. Makes 10 to 12 crepes.

Deviled Ham & Egg Crepes

Deviled ham adds spice to this egg-cheese combo.

1 (4 1/2-oz.) can deviled ham spread
8 cooked crepes
1 tablespoon butter
5 eggs
1/4 cup milk

1/2 teaspoon prepared mustard
1/2 teaspoon salt
1/8 teaspoon pepper
1 cup diced cheddar cheese
1 tablespoon melted butter

Spread about 1 tablespoon deviled ham on each cooked crepe. Melt 1 tablespoon butter in skillet. Combine eggs, milk, mustard, salt, and pepper. Pour into skillet; stir gently and cook over medium heat until eggs are set but moist. Remove from heat; add cheese. Fill crepes with egg mixture; fold over. Place in shallow baking pan. Brush with 1 tablespoon melted butter and broil until golden brown. Makes 8 crepes.

Brunch Special

Fresh vegetables really enhance the egg filling—ideal for entertaining!

Sauce:
2 tablespoons cooking oil
4 medium onions, thinly sliced
2 green peppers, thinly sliced
1/2 lb. fresh mushrooms, thinly sliced
1 clove garlic, minced
6 medium tomatoes, peeled, seeded, and chopped

1/2 teaspoon salt
1/2 teaspoon seasoned salt
1/8 teaspoon pepper
1/2 teaspoon fines herbes

Filling:
8 eggs
1/4 teaspoon salt

1/8 teaspoon pepper
2 tablespoons butter

24 cooked crepes

Sauce:
Heat oil in large saucepan; add onions and peppers. Sauté until tender. Stir in mushrooms, garlic, tomatoes, salt, seasoned salt, pepper, and fines herbes. Cover and cook 5 minutes. Uncover and cook over medium high heat for several minutes, stirring several times.

Filling:
Beat eggs, salt, and pepper. Heat butter in large skillet. Pour in egg mixture and stir with fork or wooden spoon until eggs are set but still creamy. Stir in *half* the sauce. Keep remaining sauce warm. Remove egg mixture from heat.

Spoon about 3 tablespoons filling into the center of each crepe. Fold over; place in two 13"x 9" baking pans. Cover and heat at 350°F (177°C) for 10 to 15 minutes. Spoon remaining sauce over crepes at serving time. Makes 24 crepes.

Welsh Rarebit Crepes

Use bacon or substitute imitation bacon bits.

8 strips bacon
1 tablespoon cornstarch
4 cups grated sharp cheddar cheese
1 tablespoon butter
1 cup beer
1 egg, beaten

2 teaspoons Worcestershire sauce
1 teaspoon salt
1/4 teaspoon paprika
1/4 teaspoon dry mustard
1 medium tomato, chopped
8 to 10 cooked crepes

Cook bacon until crisp. Cool, crumble and set aside. In mixing bowl combine cornstarch and cheese; set aside. In saucepan, melt butter over low heat; add beer and stir until blended. With fork, stir in cheese-cornstarch mixture; cook until cheese melts. Add beaten egg, Worcestershire sauce, salt, paprika, and mustard. Continue cooking over low heat, stirring constantly, until mixture thickens and is creamy. In shallow baking pan, fill crepes with crumbled bacon and *half* of the rarebit sauce; fold crepes over. Pour remaining sauce over all and top with chopped tomatoes. Broil until sauce is bubbly. Serve hot. Makes 8 to 10 crepes.

Egg & Chicken Liver Crepes

Similar to an omelet—wrapped in a crepe.

4 chicken livers, cut into small pieces
1 tablespoon butter
1 teaspoon Worcestershire sauce
1/4 teaspoon seasoned salt
6 eggs
1/4 cup milk

1/2 teaspoon salt
1/8 teaspoon pepper
1 tablespoon butter
8 warm cooked crepes
Paprika

Sauté chicken livers in 1 tablespoon butter. Add Worcestershire sauce and seasoned salt. Cook until livers are done; set aside and keep warm. Meantime, in small bowl, mix eggs with milk, salt, and pepper. Melt 1 tablespoon butter in skillet. Stir in eggs. Cook until set but moist. Remove from heat; add chicken livers. Fill warm cooked crepes with egg and liver mixture. Sprinkle with paprika. Serve immediately. Makes 8 crepes.

Italian Brunch Crepes

For a perfect Sunday morning!

4 eggs
1/4 cup milk
1/4 teaspoon salt
1 tablespoon butter

1/4 teaspoon mixed Italian herbs, crumbled
1/4 cup pepperoni, cut into small slivers
1 (2 1/2-oz.) can sliced mushrooms, drained
7 or 8 warm cooked crepes

Beat eggs slightly with milk and salt. Melt butter in skillet; pour in egg mixture and cook over low heat. When eggs are about half done, sprinkle with herbs and stir in pepperoni and mushrooms. Continue cooking until done. Fill cooked crepes with egg mixture. Fold over. Serve immediately. Makes 7 or 8 crepes.

Egg Crepes, East Indian Style

Add a little spice to your eggs!

5 eggs
1/4 cup milk
1/4 teaspoon salt
1/4 teaspoon curry powder

2 tablespoons butter or margarine
5 or 6 cooked crepes
2 to 3 tablespoons chutney

Beat eggs lightly with milk, salt, and curry powder. Melt butter in skillet; pour in egg mixture. Cook over low heat, stirring occasionally, until eggs are at desired degree of doneness. Fill cooked crepes with egg mixture; fold over. Spoon chutney over each folded crepe; place under broiler until bubbly. Makes 5 or 6 crepes.

CREPEWICHES

Ever tasted a crepewich? Maybe you have eaten one and didn't recognize it by that name. We coined the term, meaning foods that are usually used in making sandwiches or snacks, except crepes are used instead of bread. Doesn't that sound like fun?

Our whole family had a great time experimenting with this category. My husband thought of the *Reuben Crepes* after he ordered a Reuben Sandwich at a businessman's lunch in one of our local restaurants. *Rathskeller Crepes* is another one of his favorites because he grew up with a German background where sauerkraut and all kinds of sausages were popular fare. Naturally, the kids thought of *Pizza Crepes* because they have always enjoyed these types of foods at the fast food take-out stores.

Once you get used to this new word, you can have lots of fun making your own combinations. You might start with a mixture of the favorite foods at your home. Or, from a practical point of view, try these crepewiches as a new and unending way to disguise leftovers. Your family will be impressed with your culinary know-how.

The next time your boy or girl scout brings practically the whole hungry troop home, quickly fill them up with *Chili Dog Crepewiches*. When your mother-in-law drops in for lunch, be a gourmet show-off with *Crab Crepewiches* and she will wonder why she never appreciated you before.

Most of the crepewiches are heated with the fillings, then served open-face or folded over. If you prefer a more crispy open-face crepewich, you can heat the unfilled crepe ahead of time. Here's the best method I have found for that. Heat the oven to 325°F (163°C). On a cookie sheet, place the required number of cooked (unfilled) crepes, one layer deep, without overlapping. Bake them for about 6 to 9 minutes or until crispy. Then top with the desired ingredients.

If you want to be prepared for unexpected snackers, keep a batch of cooked, unfilled crepes in your refrigerator or freezer. This way you can be ready to make a crepewich at a moment's notice. When using a stack of unfilled crepes from your refrigerator or freezer, let them come to room temperature before separating the individual crepes—unless you used waxed paper or foil dividers.

You're on your own when selecting crepe batters for crepewiches. Mix-and-match your favorite flavors of crepe batter and filling or use ingredients that you have on hand. In most cases, it is more convenient to make a double batch of all-purpose crepes when you're cooking them for a special recipe, then freeze them for occasional crepewiches.

Reuben Crepes

A new version of a popular "Business Men's Lunch."

8 cooked crepes
1 (3-oz.) pkg. cooked, thinly sliced corned beef
1 (8-oz.) can sauerkraut, drained

1/2 teaspoon caraway seed
1/2 cup thousand island or Russian dressing
8 slices Swiss cheese

On each crepe, place sliced corned beef, sauerkraut, and caraway seed. Top filling with about 1 tablespoon dressing. Fold crepes over filling and place in shallow baking pan. Top each crepe with a slice of cheese. Heat in 350°F (177°C) oven for 15 to 20 minutes. Makes 8 crepes.

Pizza Crepes

A tasty snack with that famous Italian-American flavor!

6 cooked crepes
1 tablespoon cooking oil
1/2 cup tomato sauce
1/4 teaspoon crushed dried oregano
1/4 teaspoon crushed basil

1/3 cup pepperoni or salami, cut into thin
  strips
1 cup grated mozzarella cheese
1/4 cup grated Romano or Parmesan cheese

Brush crepes with oil, then spoon tomato sauce over. Sprinkle with oregano and basil. Top with pepperoni or salami and cheese. Broil until bubbly. Serve open-face. Makes 6 crepes. Double the recipe for a party treat.

Sloppy Joe Crepes

Messy, but good!

1 lb. lean ground beef
1 small onion, chopped
1 (10 1/2-oz.) can condensed tomato soup
1 tablespoon vinegar
1 tablespoon brown sugar
1 teaspoon chili powder

1 teaspoon Worcestershire sauce
1/4 teaspoon celery salt
1/2 teaspoon salt
10 warm cooked crepes
Cheese slices (optional)

In skillet, cook beef and onion, breaking up chunks of meat with a fork. Pour off excess grease. Stir in tomato soup, vinegar, brown sugar, chili powder, Worcestershire sauce, celery salt, and salt. Cook over moderate heat about 5 minutes. Fill crepes; fold over. Serve immediately. If desired, place one slice of cheese on each filled crepe. Place in broiler pan; broil until cheese melts. Makes 10 crepes.

All American Crepewich

Great idea for lunch or an after-the-game snack!

8 cooked crepes
8 lettuce leaves
2 large tomatoes, sliced
1 avocado, peeled and thinly sliced

8 slices bacon, cooked and crumbled
1/2 cup thousand island *or* sour cream salad
   dressing

On each crepe, arrange lettuce, then sliced tomatoes and avocados. Sprinkle bacon over top. Spoon salad dressing over all. Fold in half or serve open-face. Makes 8 crepewiches.

Rathskeller Crepes

Ideal for lunch—excellent with beer!

1 cup dairy sour cream
2 teaspoons prepared mustard
1 teaspoon horseradish
1/4 teaspoon salt

4 knockwurst or bratwurst
1 (8-oz.) can sauerkraut
8 warm Potato Crepes

In saucepan, combine sour cream, mustard, horseradish, and salt; heat but do not boil. Set aside, but keep warm. Cut knockwurst in half lengthwise; combine with sauerkraut in saucepan and simmer 5 or 6 minutes. Drain liquid from sauerkraut. Place half a knockwurst and sauerkraut in center of each crepe; fold over. Top with warm sauce; serve hot. Makes 8 crepes.

With a sharp knife, cut knockwurst or bratwurst sausage in half lengthwise so it will fit into crepe.

Spread well-drained sauerkraut along center of cooked crepe. Top with half of sausage; fold over or roll up.

Danish Crepewich

Inspired by those famous Danish open-face sandwiches.

1 (2-oz.) can anchovy fillets
1/4 cup butter
2 tablespoons Dijon mustard
4 hard-cooked eggs, finely chopped
1/2 teaspoon dried dill weed
2 teaspoons finely chopped parsley

2 teaspoons finely chopped chives
1/4 teaspoon pepper
6 cooked crepes
2 tomatoes, thinly sliced
1 cucumber, thinly sliced
Parsley or fresh dill

Drain anchovy fillets; finely chop. Mix with butter, mustard, eggs, dill, parsley, chives, and pepper. Spread over cooked crepes. Arrange sliced tomatoes and cucumbers over all. Garnish with parsley or fresh dill. Serve open-face. Makes 6 crepewiches.

Chili Dog Crepewiches

A teen-age favorite!

10 frankfurters
10 cooked crepes
1 (15-oz.) can chili with beans

1 small onion, finely chopped
2 cups grated cheddar cheese

Place one frankfurter on each cooked crepe. Top with chili with beans and onions. Fold over. Sprinkle with cheese. Place under broiler until cheese melts. Makes 10 crepewiches.

Ham-Stuffed Crepes

An old ham and egg favorite dressed up in crepes.

2 cups finely chopped cooked ham
3 hard-cooked eggs, finely chopped
2 tablespoons minced green onions
2 tablespoons chopped ripe olives
2 teaspoons sweet pickle relish

1/2 teaspoon seasoned salt
3/4 cup mayonnaise
10 cooked crepes
10 slices American or Swiss cheese

Combine ham with eggs, onions, olives, relish, seasoned salt, and mayonnaise. Spoon mixture onto cooked crepes, allowing about 3 tablespoons per crepe; fold over. Place in shallow baking pan. Arrange 1 slice cheese on each filled crepe. Broil until cheese melts. Makes 10 crepes.

Crab Crepewich

When you serve these, people will ask for your recipe.

6 ozs. fresh, frozen, or canned crab meat
1/4 cup thinly sliced green onions
1 tablespoon lemon juice
2 tablespoons chili sauce *or* cocktail sauce
5 cooked crepes

1/4 cup mayonnaise
2 egg yolks, beaten
1/3 cup grated Swiss cheese
2 egg whites

Drain and flake crab meat. In mixing bowl, combine crab with onions, lemon juice, and chili sauce or cocktail sauce. Spread on cooked crepes. Mix mayonnaise with egg yolks and cheese. Beat egg whites until firm peaks form; fold into mayonnaise mixture. Spread over crab filling on crepes. Place open-face in broiler pan; broil until bubbly and brown. Makes 5 crepewiches.

Desert Isle Crepewich

Serve these roll-ups instead of sandwiches. An especially good accompaniment to fruit or chicken salad.

1/2 cup peanut butter
1 teaspoon finely minced candied ginger
1/4 cup coconut

1/2 cup finely chopped dates
1/4 cup orange juice
5 or 6 cooked crepes

Mix peanut butter with ginger, coconut, and dates. Gradually stir in orange juice. Spread to edges of cooked crepes. Roll up like a jelly roll. Makes 5 or 6 crepe sandwiches.

VEGETABLES

Whether you're a vegetable-hater, a strict vegetarian, or somewhere in between, vegetable crepes should appeal to you. When you were a child your mother may have forced you to eat spinach or other vegetables because they "were good for you." It's true that vegetable-filled crepes are good for you, but more important, they're so good to *eat*. Some are disguised with all kinds of exciting sauces and toppings, then wrapped in a crepe to make them more palatable to vegetable cynics.

If you're a vegetarian, you'll enjoy the variety of vegetables used in crepes. Not only are individual vegetables included, but tasty combinations such as the popular *Ratatouille,* or mixtures ranging from peas and celery, to eggplant and spinach.

For all the people who need inspiration in preparing vegetables, there are vegetable crepes combined with herbs, cheese, eggs, and creamy sauces. This is an opportunity to include new versions of vegetables in menus. Vegetables dressed up in crepes seem to take on a new character and play a more important role in the meal. No longer are the vegetables "just plain boiled." Now they can borrow the foreign intrigue and mystique associated with meats and poultry. Imagine how delicious the *Green Beans with Sour Cream* would be with broiled lamb chops or *Fresh Mushroom Crepes* with broiled steaks.

I included recipes using frozen and canned vegetables as well as the fresh variety. Even though everyone enjoys garden-fresh vegetables, it is not always practical to use them. There are times when certain fresh vegetables are not available at all, and other times when they are in short supply and at such premium prices that they become budget-breakers.

If you are one of the fortunate people to have lots of garden-fresh vegetables in your backyard, you'll enjoy the *Cheese Baked Zucchini Crepes* and *Cauliflower Mornay*—as well as many other vegetable combinations. You can adapt many recipes calling for canned or frozen vegetables. If you have a good crop of asparagus or green beans, cook them and substitute them for the canned or frozen ones in the recipes.

Perhaps you have noticed that these recipes suggest you cut or slice most vegetables in fairly small pieces. This makes it easier to cut the filled crepe with a fork.

Florentine Crepes

Excellent flavor for complementing all kinds of meats. Great for a party!

2 (10-oz.) pkgs. frozen chopped spinach
1/2 teaspoon salt
1/8 teaspoon pepper
1 cup ricotta cheese
1/3 cup light cream

3 eggs, beaten slightly
1/8 teaspoon nutmeg
16 to 18 cooked crepes
2 tablespoons melted butter
1/4 cup grated Parmesan cheese

Cook spinach according to package directions; drain and *press out excess water.* Mix together spinach, salt, and pepper. Add ricotta, cream, eggs, and nutmeg. Fill crepes with spinach mixture. Roll up; place in shallow baking pan. Brush with butter; sprinkle with Parmesan cheese. Heat in 350°F (177°C) oven for 15 to 20 minutes or until hot. Makes 16 to 18 crepes.

Creamed Mushrooms

A delicious brunch treat!

2 tablespoons butter or margarine
2 tablespoons chopped onions
1 lb. fresh mushrooms, sliced
1 cup heavy cream
1/4 teaspoon seasoned salt
1/8 teaspoon pepper

2 tablespoons flour
2 tablespoons water
1/3 cup grated Gruyere cheese
8 to 10 cooked crepes
1/3 cup grated Parmesan cheese
Chopped chives

Melt butter in skillet; add onions and mushrooms. Cook over moderate heat several minutes or until mushrooms are done. Stir in cream, salt, and pepper. Lift mushrooms out of pan with slotted spoon and set aside. Dissolve flour in water; stir into creamy mixture in skillet. Simmer, stirring constantly, until thickened. Add Gruyere cheese. Meanwhile, fill crepes with cooked mushrooms; fold over. Place in shallow baking pan; spoon creamy sauce over crepes. Sprinkle with Parmesan cheese. Heat in 350°F (177°C) oven for 10 to 15 minutes. Top with chives; serve hot. Makes 8 to 10 crepes.

Fresh Mushroom Crepes

Equally good accompanying a roast beef dinner or as the main dish for brunch.

1/2 lb. fresh mushrooms
2 tablespoons butter
1/4 teaspoon salt
1/4 teaspoon seasoned salt
1 bouillon cube, crumbled

2 tablespoons dry white wine
1/2 cup dairy sour cream
1 tablespoon minced chives
7 or 8 cooked crepes

Slice mushrooms. In skillet, sauté mushrooms in butter several minutes. Add salt, seasoned salt, bouillon cube, and wine. Cook over medium heat until bubbly. Stir in sour cream and chives. Heat, but do not boil. Spoon about 3 tablespoons mushroom mixture onto center of warm crepes; fold over and serve immediately. Makes 7 or 8 crepes.

Dieter's Asparagus Cheese Crepes

High in nutrition yet relatively low in calories.

1 cup low-fat cottage cheese
1 (15-oz.) can cut asparagus, well drained
1 1/2 teaspoon instant minced onion
1 tablespoon lemon juice

1/2 teaspoon salt
6 to 8 cooked crepes
Chopped chives

In blender jar, combine cottage cheese, asparagus, onion, lemon juice, and salt; blend until smooth. Fill crepes with asparagus mixture; fold over. Place in baking dish; sprinkle with chopped chives. Cover and heat at 350°F (177°C) for 15 to 20 minutes or until hot. Makes 6 to 8 crepes.

You can substitute fresh or frozen asparagus, but be sure to cook and drain it before combining with other ingredients.

Asparagus & Egg Crepes

Hollandaise sauce makes this elegant!

1 1/2 lbs. fresh asparagus
4 eggs

6 to 8 cooked crepes
Seasoned salt

Hollandaise Sauce:
4 egg yolks
1/4 teaspoon salt
1/2 teaspoon dry mustard

1 tablespoon lemon juice
1/4 lb. butter (1 stick)

Cook asparagus in salted water; drain well. Hard cook eggs; slice. Arrange eggs and asparagus on crepes. Sprinkle with seasoned salt. Fold crepes over. Place in shallow baking pan; cover with foil. Heat in 350°F (177°C) oven about 10 minutes or until warm.

Sauce:
Put egg yolks, salt, mustard, and lemon juice in blender. Cover and blend on low until eggs are well mixed. Heat butter until melted and bubbly hot. Immediately, pour butter in steady stream through small hole in top of blender, keeping blender on low until mixture is thickened. Spoon sauce over warm filled crepes. Serve immediately. Makes 6 to 8 crepes.

Asparagus Crepes Au Gratin

Glamorize asparagus this easy way.

2 (8-oz.) pkgs. frozen asparagus
12 or 13 cooked crepes
Salt and pepper
1 (10 1/2-oz.) can cream of asparagus soup,
    undiluted

1/4 cup milk or light cream
1/2 cup grated sharp cheddar cheese

Cook asparagus according to package directions; drain thoroughly. Place several stalks across center of each cooked crepe. Sprinkle with salt and pepper; roll up. Place in shallow baking pan. Combine soup with milk. Spoon over filled crepes. Sprinkle with cheese. Broil until bubbly. Makes 12 or 13 crepes.

Broccoli Au Gratin

Try this for a dinner party.

2 (10-oz.) pkgs. frozen chopped broccoli
3 slices bacon, chopped
2 tablespoons flour
3/4 cup light cream
1/2 cup chicken bouillon

1/2 teaspoon salt
1/8 teaspoon pepper
12 to 14 cooked crepes
1/2 cup soft bread crumbs
2 tablespoons melted butter

Cook broccoli according to package directions; drain well. Meanwhile, in saucepan, cook bacon. Stir in flour, then cream, bouillon, salt, and pepper. Cook over low heat, stirring constantly, until thickened. Stir in cooked, drained broccoli. Fill crepes with broccoli mixture. Sprinkle combination of bread crumbs and melted butter over each. Place in broiler until bread crumbs begin to brown. Makes 12 to 14 crepes.

Golden Cauliflower Cups

Wonderful flavor surprise of cauliflower with cheese and ham.

12 cooked crepes
2 cups cooked, chopped cauliflower
  (1 small head)
1/2 cup chopped ham
1/2 cup grated cheddar cheese

1 1/2 cups light cream
3 egg yolks, slightly beaten
2 tablespoons flour
1/2 teaspoon salt

Line greased muffin pans with cooked crepes. Arrange cauliflower, ham, and cheese in each cup. Combine cream, egg yolks, flour, and salt; beat until smooth. Pour over cauliflower mixture. Bake at 350°F (177°C) for 15 to 20 minutes or until firm. Makes 12 cups.

Cauliflower Mornay Crepes

Exceptional in flavor and texture!

1 small head cauliflower (about 2 cups)
3 tablespoons butter
3 tablespoons flour
1/2 cup light cream
1/2 cup milk

1/2 teaspoon salt
8 cooked crepes
1/2 cup soft bread crumbs
1 tablespoon melted butter
1/4 cup grated cheddar cheese

Break cauliflower into small pieces. Cook in salted water until tender; drain thoroughly. Meanwhile, melt butter; stir in flour. Then add cream, milk, and salt. Cook over low heat, stirring until thickened. Combine with cauliflower. Fill crepes; fold over. Place in baking pan. Mix bread crumbs with butter and cheese. Sprinkle over crepes. Heat in 350°F (177°C) oven about 15 to 20 minutes. Makes 8 crepes.

Scalloped Zucchini

A great way to use your garden vegetables.

1 carrot, thinly sliced
2 tablespoons chopped onion
2 tablespoons chopped green pepper
1/2 cup sliced celery
1/4 cup water
2 medium zucchini, thinly sliced

1 tomato, chopped
1/2 teaspoon salt
1/8 teaspoon pepper
1/4 teaspoon basil leaves, crushed
8 to 10 warm cooked crepes

Sauce:
1 (3-oz.) pkg. cream cheese
2 tablespoons milk

1 egg yolk
1 teaspoon lemon juice

In saucepan, combine carrot with onion, green pepper, celery, and water. Cover and cook about 5 minutes; drain. Stir in zucchini, tomato, salt, pepper, and basil. Cook another 5 minutes or until vegetables are tender. Fill crepes; fold over. Place on broiler pan. Meanwhile, make sauce by mixing cream cheese with milk, egg yolk, and lemon juice. Spoon over filled crepes. Broil until bubbly and golden brown. Makes 8 to 10 crepes.

Cheese Baked Zucchini Crepes

The greatest vegetable dish!

2 tablespoons chopped onion
2 tablespoons butter
1 1/2 lbs. zucchini, sliced
1/2 cup water
1 egg, slightly beaten

1/2 teaspoon salt
2/3 cup grated sharp cheddar cheese
10 to 12 cooked crepes
1/2 cup soft bread crumbs
2 tablespoons melted butter

Briefly sauté onion in butter. Stir in zucchini and water. Cover and simmer 10 to 15 minutes or until zucchini is soft. Drain thoroughly. With electric mixer on low speed, break up zucchini into small pieces; drain off any excess water. Stir in beaten egg. Add salt and cheese. Line buttered custard cups or muffin pans with cooked crepes. Spoon zucchini mixture into center of each. Combine bread crumbs with butter. Sprinkle over filling. Bake in 350°F (177°C) oven for 15 to 20 minutes. Makes 10 to 12 cups.

Green Beans Oriental

Zesty flavor with mushroom and onion.

1 (16-oz.) can French-style green beans or
   fresh beans
2 tablespoons butter or margarine
1 tablespoon instant minced onion
1 cup fresh bean sprouts
1 (8 1/2-oz.) can water chestnuts, drained and sliced

1 (10 1/2-oz.) can condensed cream of
   mushroom soup
1/2 cup milk
10 to 12 cooked crepes

Drain canned beans; or cook fresh beans, drain and set aside. Melt butter in skillet; add onion, bean sprouts, and water chestnuts. Cover pan and cook several minutes. Add cooked, drained beans. Fill cooked crepes with vegetables. Mix condensed soup and milk. Spoon about a tablespoon of soup over the vegetables in each crepe. Fold over. Place in shallow baking pan; pour remaining soup mixture over all. Heat in 350°F (177°C) oven for 15 to 20 minutes. Makes 10 to 12 crepes.

Ratatouille Crepes

The "in" vegetable dish!

1 lb. zucchini
1 small eggplant
1 onion, sliced
1/4 cup cooking oil or butter
1 clove garlic, minced
2 tomatoes, peeled and chopped
1 green pepper, chopped

1 teaspoon salt
1/8 teaspoon pepper
1/4 teaspoon basil leaves, crumbled
1/4 teaspoon thyme leaves, crumbled
20 to 22 warm cooked crepes
Chopped parsley

Cut zucchini and eggplant into 1/2-inch cubes. In large skillet, sauté zucchini, eggplant, and onion in oil or butter. Stir in garlic, tomatoes, green pepper, salt, pepper, basil, and thyme. Cook, covered, on medium heat 10 to 15 minutes or until vegetables are tender. Fill warm crepes; fold over. Sprinkle with chopped parsley and serve immediately. Makes 20 to 22 crepes.

Using a sharp knife on a cutting board, chop zucchini and eggplant into 1/2-inch cubes.

In large skillet, combine cubed zucchini and eggplant with onion slices in cooking oil.

Spoon cooked vegetables along center of warm cooked crepes; fold over both sides and sprinkle with chopped parsley.

Green Beans with Sour Cream

You'll love these!

1 tablespoon butter or margarine
1 tablespoon flour
1/4 teaspoon salt
1/2 teaspoon grated onion
1/8 teaspoon pepper
1/2 teaspoon grated lemon peel
1/4 cup water

1/2 cup dairy sour cream
1 (16-oz.) can French-style green beans, drained
6 to 8 cooked crepes
1/4 cup grated cheddar cheese
1 tablespoon melted butter
1/4 cup dry bread crumbs

In saucepan, melt 1 tablespoon butter; stir in flour, salt, onion, pepper, and lemon peel. Mix in water; cook until thick. Stir in sour cream, then green beans. Fill crepes; fold over. Mix cheese with 1 tablespoon melted butter and bread crumbs. Sprinkle over filled crepes. Place in broiler until cheese melts. Makes 6 to 8 crepes.

Vegetable Melange with Cheese Sauce

A vegetable-lovers crepe. Recipe makes enough for a party.

1 small eggplant, cut into 1/2-inch chunks
1 small onion, chopped
2 tablespoons cooking oil
1 bunch spinach, washed and drained
2 tomatoes, diced

1/2 teaspoon salt
1/8 teaspoon pepper
1/4 teaspoon dried basil leaves, crumbled
15 or 16 warm cooked crepes

Egg Sauce:
2 tablespoons butter or margarine
2 tablespoons flour
1 cup milk

1/4 teaspoon salt
1/8 teaspoon dry mustard
3 hard-cooked eggs, peeled and diced

In skillet, sauté eggplant and onions in oil several minutes. Stir in spinach, tomatoes, salt, pepper, and basil. Cover and simmer until vegetables are tender. Fill crepes; fold over. Spoon egg sauce over; serve immediately. Makes 15 or 16 crepes.

Egg Sauce:
Melt butter in small saucepan; stir in flour. Add milk, salt, and mustard. Cook over low heat, stirring constantly, until thickened. Add eggs. Serve over filled crepes.

Vegetable Medley

Appetizing vegetable combination!

2 cups zucchini, cut into 1/2-inch cubes
1 (10-oz.) pkg. frozen peas, thawed
1/2 cup sliced celery
1/4 cup chopped onion
1/4 cup butter or margarine

1/4 teaspoon salt
1/4 teaspoon oregano, crushed
1/8 teaspoon garlic salt
12 to 14 cooked crepes
1/4 cup grated Parmesan cheese

In large skillet, sauté zucchini, peas, celery, and onion in butter for 8 to 10 minutes or until vegetables are tender. Cover pan part of the cooking time. Stir in salt, oregano, and garlic salt. Fill crepes; fold over. Place in shallow baking pan. Sprinkle with cheese. Heat in 350°F (177°C) oven for 10 to 15 minutes. Makes 12 to 14 crepes.

Garden Crepes

Hearty vegetable combo!

Filling:
1/4 cup butter
1/2 cup dry bread crumbs
1 tablespoon chopped parsley
1/2 teaspoon salt
1/8 teaspoon pepper

2 tablespoons sherry wine
2 hard-cooked eggs, chopped
1 cup chopped cooked carrots
1 cup chopped cooked cauliflower

11 or 12 cooked crepes

Sauce:
2 tablespoons butter
2 tablespoons flour
1/4 teaspoon salt
1/8 teaspoon pepper

1 cup milk
1 cup grated cheddar cheese
1 teaspoon dry mustard
1/2 teaspoon Worcestershire sauce

Filling:
Melt butter in saucepan; add bread crumbs. Cook until light brown. Stir in parsley, salt, pepper, wine, eggs, carrots, and cauliflower. Fill cooked crepes with vegetables; fold over. Heat in 350°F (177°C) oven for 15 to 20 minutes. Serve with cheese sauce. Makes 11 or 12 crepes.

Sauce:
Melt butter in saucepan over low heat. Blend in flour, salt, and pepper. Cook over low heat, stirring until mixture is smooth and bubbly. Remove from heat; stir in milk. Heat to boiling. Add remaining ingredients, stirring constantly, until cheese is melted. Serve hot over crepes.

APPETIZERS

Appetizers get your meal off to the right start. And they're an essential ingredient for a superb party.

Crepe appetizers may be new to you, but it won't take long to get used to them. There's a flavor and shape to suit every taste and occasion.

Crepe batter is the starting point. Naturally, all-purpose batters may be used for any appetizers; or you might enjoy trying herb, wheat germ or beer batter for variety.

If you make up any of these batters for other dishes, and have cooked unfilled crepes left over, be sure to save them for appetizers. They are bite-size so lots of them can be made out of a very few crepes. Most appetizers can be filled and then refrigerated several hours or overnight to avoid last-minute preparation.

Appetizer crepes come in a variety of shapes and that's part of the fun. You can spread them with the filling and roll them up like miniature jelly rolls. These are usually easier to cut if they are chilled and then cut into 4 or 5 pieces crosswise. Serve them alone on an appetizer tray or combine an appetizer on a toothpick with an olive, cherry tomato or cocktail onion. For a change, spread the filling on each crepe, then cut each one into about 10 or 12 small wedges; roll up each little wedge like a crescent roll. One of the most dramatic shapes is a crepe stack. A number of crepes—usually 5 to 8—are spread with a filling and stacked one on top of another; topped with chopped nuts or parsley, then chilled and cut into small wedges.

To heat or not to heat, is the debatable question about crepe appetizers. It's often a matter of personal preferences. Some appetizers can be popped into the oven or broiled at the last minute. I like to heat them in the microwave oven because it does the job so quickly. So, if you have a microwave, just follow the manufacturer's directions for heating traditional appetizers. Remember that it takes only a minute or two and sometimes, less than that!

Appetizers aren't always colorful by themselves, dress them up for the party. Popular festive garnishes are small strips of pimiento, minced parsley, watercress, sliced olives, chopped egg or anchovies.

Party Wedges

Make ahead and refrigerate until party time.

1/2 cup chopped pecans
1/4 teaspoon salt
2 tablespoons butter
1 (8-oz.) pkg. cream cheese, softened
2 teaspoons milk
1 tablespoon grated onion

1/2 teaspoon garlic salt
1/4 teaspoon black pepper
1/2 cup dairy sour cream
1 (2 1/2-oz.) pkg. dried beef, finely chopped
1/4 cup finely chopped green pepper
10 cooked crepes

In small skillet, combine pecans with salt and butter. Cook over medium heat until golden brown, stirring several times; set aside. In small mixing bowl, mix cream cheese with milk, onion, garlic salt, black pepper, and sour cream until smooth. Stir in beef and green pepper. Spread 2 to 3 tablespoons beef mixture over each crepe. Make 2 stacks, each 5 crepes high. Sprinkle toasted pecans on top. Refrigerate at least 1 hour. Cut into wedges for appetizer servings. Makes 16 to 20 wedges.

Finely chop the beef before adding to softened cream cheese and seasonings.

Spread filling over each crepe; then stack crepes on top of each other.

Refrigerate each stack for easy cutting. At serving time, cut small wedges for individual appetizers.

Cheese & bacon Rolls

Make ahead and refrigerate until cocktail time.

1/2 lb. sharp cheddar cheese
6 slices bacon, cooked
1 small onion
1 teaspoon dry mustard

1/2 teaspoon Worcestershire sauce
2 teaspoons mayonnaise
15 cooked crepes
Melted butter

Put cheese, cooked bacon, and onion through food grinder. Stir in mustard, Worcestershire sauce, and mayonnaise. Form cheese mixture into 5 rolls about 1/2 inch in diameter and 12 inches long. Cut each roll into three pieces about 4 inches long. Place one piece of cheese mixture in center of each cooked crepe. Roll up; chill. Just before serving place in broiler pan; brush with butter. Broil until bubbly. Cut each crepe into 4 crosswise pieces. Serve warm. Makes 15 rolls or 60 appetizers.

Variation:
Instead of broiling the filled crepes, brush all sides of crepes with milk; roll in dry bread crumbs and brown in butter in large skillet. Cut each crepe into 4 pieces and serve warm.

Smoked Oyster Appetizers

A versatile appetizer—equally good hot or cold.

1 (3-oz.) pkg. cream cheese, softened
2 tablespoons mayonnaise
1 tablespoon finely chopped chives
1 teaspoon finely chopped pimiento

1 (3 1/2-oz.) can smoked oysters, drained and
  chopped
4 or 5 cooked crepes

Combine cream cheese with mayonnaise, chives, pimiento, and oysters. Spread on cooked crepes. Cut each crepe into 6 wedges. Roll up each piece like a crescent roll. Serve cold; or broil until bubbly and serve hot. Makes 24 to 30 appetizers.

Pineapple Cheese Appetizers

A surprise combination for your next party.

2 cups grated sharp cheddar cheese
1 (8-oz.) pkg. cream cheese, softened
1 (8 1/4-oz.) can crushed pineapple,
  drained thoroughly

3 slices bacon, cooked and crumbled
2 tablespoons minced green pepper
14 to 16 cooked crepes

In medium mixing bowl, mix cheddar and cream cheese. Stir in pineapple, bacon, and green pepper. Spread about 2 tablespoons filling on each crepe. Roll up like a jelly roll. Refrigerate several hours. Cut each crepe crosswise into 8 to 10 slices. Makes about 150 appetizers.

Cheese Olive Snack

These appetizers are sure to disappear immediately!

2 cups grated sharp cheddar cheese
1 (4 1/2-oz.) can ripe olives, drained
  and chopped
2 tablespoons finely chopped green onions

1 cup mayonnaise
15 cooked crepes
Imitation bacon bits or crumbled cooked bacon

Combine cheese with olives, onions, and mayonnaise. Spread on cooked crepes. Broil until bubbly; sprinkle with bacon bits. Cut each into 5 or 6 wedges; serve hot. Makes 75 to 90 appetizers.

Appetizer Dippin' Chips

Pick out your favorite combination of flavors. Select one or more of these suggestions and look through your spice collection for other ideas.

6 cooked crepes
Melted butter

Suggested Seasonings:
Seasoned salt
Garlic salt
Dried dill weed

Mexican seasoning
Grated Parmesan cheese

Brush crepes with butter; sprinkle with one or more of the suggested seasonings. Cut each cooked crepe into quarters, then each quarter into 3 or 4 wedges, forming 12 to 16 pieces. Place on cookie sheet. Bake in 325°F (163°C) oven for 6 to 9 minutes or until crispy. Makes 72 to 96 dippers.

Hot Chili Roquefort Roll-ups

Whip up this hot appetizer on a moment's notice.

1 oz. crumbled Roquefort cheese
1 (3-oz.) pkg. cream cheese, softened
1 tablespoon catsup
1 teaspoon chili powder

1/4 teaspoon paprika
1/16 teaspoon garlic powder
4 cooked crepes

Blend Roquefort and cream cheese with catsup, chili powder, paprika, and garlic powder. Spread over cooked crepes. Broil until bubbly. Gently roll up each broiled crepe like a jelly roll. Cut each roll-up into 5 pieces. Serve hot. Makes 20 appetizers.

Cheese Whirls

Slightly messy to eat but well worth the inconvenience!

1 tablespoon butter, softened
1 cup grated Monterey Jack cheese
1 tablespoon horseradish
1/4 teaspoon salt

1/4 teaspoon paprika
1 tablespoon minced green onion
1 egg white
5 cooked crepes

Mix butter with cheese, horseradish, salt, paprika, and green onion. Stir in unbeaten egg white. Spread about 2 tablespoons of mixture on each cooked crepe. Roll up; chill for several hours. Cut each rolled crepe crosswise into 5 or 6 slices. Bake on cookie sheet in 425°F (218°C) oven for 5 or 6 minutes, or broil until bubbly. Makes about 25 to 30 appetizers.

Appetizer Tray.
Left to right: Smoked Oyster Appetizers,
Cheese & Bacon Rolls, Party Wedges.

Curried Tuna Appetizers

A great appetizer with subtle curry flavor.

1 (7-oz.) can tuna, drained
1/4 teaspoon salt
1/2 teaspoon curry powder
3 tablespoons mayonnaise

1 teaspoon lemon juice
2 teaspoons instant minced onion
6 cooked crepes
Pimiento strips

Break tuna into small pieces. Add salt, curry, mayonnaise, lemon juice, and onion. Spread on cooked crepes; roll up. Refrigerate until serving time. Cut each crepe into 4 pieces. Garnish with pimiento strips. Makes 24 appetizers.

Seafood Hors D'Oeuvres

A different kind of appetizer!

1 teaspoon chopped chives
1/8 teaspoon dried tarragon leaves, crumbled
2 teaspoons chopped parsley
1/8 teaspoon dried chervil leaves, crumbled

1/8 teaspoon dried dill weed
1 cup mayonnaise
8 cooked crepes
1/2 lb. small shrimp, cooked and shelled

Combine herbs with mayonnaise. Let stand at least an hour if possible. Spread on cooked crepes. Cut each crepe into 8 wedges. Place 1 shrimp on each wedge. Roll up like a crescent roll. Makes 64 appetizers. Serve individually or arrange on a toothpick with an olive or cube of avocado.

Smoked Salmon Rolls

A terrific make-ahead appetizer!

1 (3-oz.) pkg. cream cheese
2 tablespoons dairy sour cream
1/8 teaspoon salt
1/8 teaspoon pepper
1 tablespoon minced chives

1 tablespoon horseradish
6 cooked crepes
6 very thin slices smoked salmon (lox)
Paprika

Mix cream cheese with sour cream, salt, pepper, chives, and horseradish. Spread on cooked crepes. Place thin slice of salmon over each. Roll up like jelly roll. Refrigerate until serving time. Slice each filled crepe into 4 or 5 crosswise pieces. Sprinkle with paprika. Makes 24 to 30 appetizers.

Chicken Liver Appetizers

Make chicken-liver mixture ahead and spread it on crepes just before party time.

1/2 pound chicken livers
1/4 cup butter
1 onion, chopped
1 clove garlic, minced
1/2 teaspoon salt

1/4 teaspoon pepper
1/8 teaspoon dried oregano leaves
1/8 teaspoon dried tarragon leaves
1 tablespoon brandy
5 cooked crepes

In skillet, sauté livers in butter; stir in onions and cook several minutes. Add garlic, salt, pepper, oregano, and tarragon. Cover and simmer 2 or 3 minutes. Pour in brandy. Place in blender; purée until almost smooth. Chill. Spread on cooked crepes. Cut each crepe into 10 to 12 wedges; roll up each wedge like a crescent roll. Makes 50 to 60 appetizers.

Caviar Appetizers

A real delicacy!

6 cooked crepes
1 small jar caviar
4 hard-cooked eggs

1 onion, finely chopped
1 lemon, cut into small wedges

Cut each crepe into 10 to 12 small wedges. Place on cookie sheet. Bake in 325°F (163°C) oven for about 8 to 10 minutes or until chips are golden brown. Cool. Spoon caviar into small bowl. Separate hard-cooked egg yolks and whites; chop each. Put yolks in one small bowl and whites in another. Place onion in another small bowl, and lemon in still another. Arrange all bowls on tray. Surround bowls with crepe chips. Let each person spoon caviar on crepe chips, seasoning with other ingredients as desired.

As a substitute for this caviar appetizer tray, you might try the crisp crepe chips around small separate bowls of cheese spread, chopped olives, green chile peppers, sliced mushrooms, and crumbled cooked bacon. Then each person can dip 'n mix chips with any of the accompaniments.

DESSERTS

The magnificent crepe really gained its notoriety from the "goodies" that grace its fold. Dessert crepes have been served in famous restaurants 'round the world and relished by gourmets for many years. These associations have given the dessert crepe—especially flaming ones—a mysterious, almost forbidding air. Yet, in reality, there is nothing special or complicated about concocting them. Take the suzette—making the crepe, the sauce and flaming it is far less complex than preparing a lemon meringue pie. Let me assure you: This myth of complexity has been greatly overdone.

Dessert-crepe batters are recommended for preparing dessert crepes. But, if your refrigerator or freezer contains crepes made from all-purpose batter, don't hesitate to use them in preparing dessert crepes. The lack of sweetness in the crepe batter will be hard to detect because the sauce or filling flavor permeates the final dish.

A word about the "mysteries" of flaming crepes. Don't miss out on the glory of this type of dessert presentation because you are concerned about the flaming process. A few simple techniques will ensure a successful and safe operation:

Heating the liqueur—Liqueur with a high alcohol content (proof) will flame quite high if hot when ignited. Therefore, the rule is: *The higher the proof, the lower the liqueur's temperature needs to be when ignited.* A 35-proof liqueur should be very hot—but not boiling—when ignited. 80-proof should be warm. Proportionate temperatures should be used for other proofs. It is difficult to flame liqueurs below 35-proof.

Igniting the liqueur—I prefer to use a long fireplace match. This adds flair and enhances safety. Be sure there is no combustible material above or near the pan.

Basting the crepes—Wait until the flames die down enough to be out of finger range before spooning hot sauce over the crepes. Be sure *all* flames are out before serving the crepes.

Don't hesitate to flambé because you don't happen to have a crepe-finishing pan. Any skillet or shallow, wide-bottom pan will do just fine. Some of my friends use chafing dishes.

Dessert crepes are a delectable finale to your meal, lending grace and the gourmet touch. Serve them often!

Apple Crepes with Cheese

Reminds you of old-fashioned apple pie with cheese.

3/4 cup water
3/4 cup sugar
1/4 teaspoon cinnamon
5 cooking apples, peeled, cored, and sliced

10 cooked crepes
1 (3-oz.) pkg. cream cheese, softened
1/2 cup grated sharp cheddar cheese
1/2 cup dairy sour cream

Bring water, sugar, and cinnamon to boil in saucepan. Add apples, simmering until tender. Drain; save syrup. Fill crepes with drained apples; fold over. Place in skillet or chafing dish; pour syrup from apples over crepes. Heat to boiling. Meanwhile, beat cream cheese with cheddar cheese until smooth; stir in sour cream. Serve with hot crepes. Makes 10 crepes.

Red-Hot Apple Crepes

Popular red-hot cinnamon candies make these crepes colorful and spicy!

2 cups water
1/2 cup sugar
1/2 cup red-hot cinnamon candies
4 apples, peeled, cored, and thinly sliced
2 (3-oz.) pkgs. cream cheese, softened

1/4 cup milk
1/4 cup finely chopped walnuts
12 cooked crepes
2 tablespoons cornstarch
2 tablespoons cold water

In saucepan, bring water and sugar to boil. Pour in candies; stir until melted. Add apples; cover and simmer about 10 minutes or until tender. Let apples stand in sauce until deep pink, turning if necessary for uniform color. Meanwhile, mix softened cream cheese with milk and walnuts; spread on cooked crepes. Drain apples, saving sauce. Dissolve cornstarch in cold water; stir into apple syrup while heating for several minutes until thickened and translucent. Place apple slices on top of cream cheese filling; fold crepes over. Serve with sauce. Makes 12 crepes.

Würzburg Crepes

Like peanut flavor? This is the ultimate!

1 (8-oz.) can applesauce
1/4 cup peanut butter
1 cup powdered sugar
1/2 tablespoon powdered cinnamon

10 cooked crepes
1 tablespoon butter
1/4 cup rum *or* almond-flavored Italian liqueur

In small mixing bowl, combine applesauce and peanut butter thoroughly. In another small mixing bowl, combine powdered sugar and cinnamon. Spoon 2 tablespoons applesauce mixture and 1 tablespoon sugar mixture in center of each crepe. Set aside remaining sugar mixture. Fold bottom up, sides in, top down for blintz shape. Refrigerate until needed. At serving time, melt butter in chafing dish or crepe pan; arrange crepes folded edges down in pan. Sprinkle crepes with remaining sugar mixture. Cook on low heat for about 1 minute. Pour rum or almond-flavored Italian liqueur over crepes and ignite with long match. Gently slide pan back and forth over heat and spoon sauce over crepes until flames die. Place crepes in serving dishes; spoon hot sauce over crepes. Serve immediately. Makes 10 crepes.

Swedish Apple Stack

An idea borrowed from the famous Swedish apple cake.

3 medium cooking apples
2 tablespoons butter or margarine
1/3 cup sugar
1 tablespoon cornstarch
1 tablespoon water
5 zwieback, crushed (about 1/2 cup)

1/2 teaspoon ground cinnamon
1 tablespoon brown sugar
8 cooked crepes
1 cup dairy sour cream
2 tablespoons finely chopped pecans

Peel, core, and finely chop apples. Melt butter in skillet; stir in apples and sugar. Cover and cook over moderate heat for about 10 minutes, stirring frequently, until apples start to soften. Dissolve cornstarch in water. Add to apples. Cook over low heat, stirring constantly, until slightly thickened. Set aside. Finely crush zwieback; mix with cinnamon and brown sugar. Onto one cooked crepe spoon some apple mixture, then about 2 tablespoons sour cream, and some of the crumb mixture. Repeat with remaining crepes, stacking one on top of the other. Spread remaining sour cream over top layer. Sprinkle with nuts. Chill several hours. Cut into 6 or 8 pie-shaped wedges.

Strudel-Style Apple Crepes

A quickie dessert that's simply delicious!

1 (16-oz.) can applesauce
10 to 12 cooked crepes
1/3 cup melted butter

2 tablespoons granulated sugar
3 tablespoons powdered sugar
Cinnamon

Spread 2 to 3 tablespoons of applesauce over each crepe leaving 1/2-inch border; roll up. Brush with melted butter. Pour remaining butter in hot skillet or chafing dish. Place filled crepes in skillet. Sprinkle with granulated sugar. Heat until lightly browned on all sides. Serve hot. Sprinkle with powdered sugar and cinnamon. Makes 10 to 12 crepes.

Peaches Flambé

A flaming beauty!

1/4 cup butter
1 (1-lb.) can sliced peaches
1/2 cup orange juice
1 teaspoon grated orange peel

1 tablespoon sugar
1/4 cup brandy, heated
8 warm cooked crepes, folded into quarters
1/4 cup chopped pecans (optional)

Melt butter in skillet or chafing dish. Drain peaches; save juice. Combine peach juice (about 3/4 cup) with orange juice; pour in pan with butter. Simmer about 5 minutes or until slightly thickened. Stir in peaches. Sprinkle with orange peel and sugar. Pour in warm brandy. Ignite with long match. When flames die, spoon peaches and sauce over warm crepes on individual dessert plates. Sprinkle with pecans if desired. Makes 8 crepes.

Classic Crepes Suzette

A traditional French suzette recipe.

6 small sugar cubes
1 lemon
1 large orange
1/2 cup sweet butter, softened

1 tablespoon granulated sugar
10 to 12 cooked Dessert Crepes
1/4 cup Grand Marnier
2 tablespoons dark rum

Rub 3 sugar cubes on surface of whole unpeeled lemon, turn each cube to coat it on all sides. Then rub remaining 3 cubes on whole unpeeled orange. Set aside. Squeeze orange; strain juice—should be about 1/2 cup. Drop all 6 cubes into orange juice; mash and stir until dissolved. In small deep bowl, cream butter with 1 tablespoon sugar; cover and refrigerate until needed. At serving time, warm creamed butter in chafing dish or crepe finishing pan. Add orange-juice mixture; cook briskly, stirring often—about 4 minutes or until sauce thickens. Place cooked crepes in sauce; quickly turn each crepe and fold into quarters. Move folded crepes to side of pan and arrange in overlapping circle as they are sauced. Carefully pour Grand Marnier and rum into center of pan. Ignite with long match. Gently slide the pan back and forth over the heat and spoon sauce over crepes until flames die. Serve at once. Makes 5 or 6 servings of two crepes per person.

Holding whole unpeeled orange in one hand and sugar cube in other, gently rub all sides of cube over surface of orange. Repeat procedure with lemon.

After rubbing sugar cubes on orange and lemon, drop into orange juice; mash with back of a spoon.

In chafing dish or crepe finishing pan, melt creamed butter; then pour in orange-juice mixture, stirring until well blended.

Gently place cooked crepes into hot orange mixture after it is slightly thickened.

With wooden spoon in each hand, quickly fold each crepe in half; then half again, forming a triangle shape. With spoon, push crepes to side of pan after they have been folded and coated with sauce.

Peaches & Cream

Equally good with strawberries or nectarines.

4 large fresh peaches, peeled and sliced
2 tablespoons sugar
1 (14-oz.) can sweetened *condensed* milk
1/4 cup lemon juice

1/2 cup heavy cream, whipped
8 to 10 cooked crepes
Whipped cream (optional)

Sprinkle peaches with sugar; set aside. In medium bowl, beat sweetened condensed milk with lemon juice until thick. Fold in whipped cream and sweetened peaches. Fill cooked crepes; fold over. Serve with additional whipped cream, if desired. Makes 8 to 10 crepes.

Brandied Peach Crepes with Almond Sauce

A delicious way to serve fresh peaches!

3 or 4 large fresh peaches
1/4 cup sugar
2 tablespoons peach brandy

10 to 12 cooked crepes
1/4 cup toasted slivered almonds

Sauce:
1/2 cup sugar
1/4 teaspoon salt
2 tablespoons cornstarch
2 cups light cream

2 egg yolks, beaten
1 tablespoon butter or margarine
1/2 teaspoon almond extract

Peel and thinly slice peaches. In small bowl, combine with sugar and brandy. Spoon onto crepes. Fold over. Serve with sauce. Makes 10 to 12 crepes.

Sauce:
Mix sugar, salt, and cornstarch in saucepan. Gradually stir in cream. Cook over medium heat, stirring constantly, until mixture thickens. Remove from heat; gradually stir part of hot mixture into beaten egg yolks. Return egg mixture to saucepan. Simmer, stirring, for 1 minute. Remove from heat. Stir in butter and almond extract. Serve warm or cool over peach crepes.

Apricot Walnut Crepes

Rich walnut filling enhanced by an apricot topping.

1 cup ground walnuts
3/4 cup powdered sugar
1 teaspoon brandy
1 cup dairy sour cream

1/2 teaspoon vanilla
12 to 14 cooked crepes
3/4 cup apricot preserves
Powdered sugar

Combine walnuts with 3/4 cup sugar, brandy, sour cream, and vanilla. Spread on cooked crepes. Roll up or fold over. Spoon apricot preserves over top. Sprinkle with additional powdered sugar. These may be prepared just before dinner and set aside until dessert time. Makes 12 to 14 crepes.

Apricot Crepes Flambé

An elegant grand finale to any meal!

1 (17-oz.) can apricot halves
1 teaspoon grated orange peel
2 tablespoons butter

10 cooked crepes
2 tablespoons sugar
1/4 cup orange-flavored liqueur, warmed

Drain apricots, saving 1 cup syrup. In skillet or chafing dish, heat 1 cup syrup with orange peel and butter until butter is melted. Place 1 apricot half on each cooked crepe; fold over. Arrange apricot-filled crepes in hot apricot sauce. Heat to boiling. Sprinkle with sugar; pour in liqueur. Ignite with long match. Spoon sauce over crepes until flame burns out. Serve immediately. Makes 10 crepes.

Crepes Suzette Americana

An excellent crepe suzette.

1/2 lb. unsalted butter, softened
1/2 cup sugar
1 teaspoon lemon juice
1/2 cup orange juice
1/4 cup orange liqueur

1 tablespoon grated orange peel
16 to 18 cooked crepes
2 tablespoons sugar
1/4 cup orange liqueur
1/4 cup cognac

Beat butter with 1/2 cup sugar until very creamy. Slowly add lemon juice, orange juice and 1/4 cup liqueur while beating. Stir in orange peel. Refrigerate until needed. At serving time, heat orange butter in skillet or chafing dish until bubbly. Dip both sides of crepe in hot orange butter and fold over or roll up; push over to edge of chafing dish. Repeat with remaining crepes. Sprinkle crepes with 2 tablespoons sugar; pour 1/4 cup liqueur and 1/4 cup cognac into center of pan. With long match, ignite mixture. Shake chafing dish or skillet with one hand, and with the other, spoon flaming sauce over crepes. When flames die out, quickly serve crepes on heated dessert plates; spoon sauce over. Makes 16 to 18 crepes.

Quick Crepes Suzette

An excellent short-cut version of the traditional recipe.

1/2 cup sweet butter, softened
1/4 cup sugar
2 teaspoons grated orange peel
1/2 cup orange juice

1 teaspoon lemon juice
10 to 12 cooked crepes
1/4 cup orange-flavored liqueur
2 tablespoons apricot or peach brandy

Cream butter; gradually beat in sugar. Add orange peel, orange juice, and lemon juice. Heat in skillet or chafing dish. Dip cooked crepes in mixture; fold or roll them and move to side of pan. Heat liqueur and brandy in small pan. Pour over crepes; ignite with long match. Spoon sauce over crepes until flames die. Serve immediately. Makes 5 or 6 servings.

Classic Crepes Suzette

Quick Apricot Crepes

Vary this filling with your favorite jam.

12 cooked crepes
1/2 cup apricot jam
2 tablespoons sugar

2 tablespoons melted butter
1/4 cup apricot brandy

Spread cooked crepes with jam. Roll up; arrange in buttered baking dish and sprinkle with sugar and melted butter. Place under broiler long enough to lightly brown the top. Heat brandy in small pan; pour over hot crepes. Ignite with long match. Serve immediately. Makes 12 crepes.

Crepes Luau

A flaming Polynesian delight!

1 (15 1/4-oz.) can crushed pineapple, drained
1 tablespoon brown sugar
3/4 cup coconut
3 tablespoons rum

8 cooked crepes
3 tablespoons butter
1/4 cup rum, warmed

Combine drained pineapple with brown sugar, coconut, and 3 tablespoons rum. Place about 2 tablespoons of the mixture in center of each cooked crepe. Fold bottom of crepe over filling; then both sides and finally the top. In skillet or chafing dish, lightly brown the crepes in butter. Pour 1/4 cup rum over crepes and ignite with long match. Serve immediately. Makes 8 crepes.

Strawberries Romanoff

Cream topping is slightly runny and really good!

2 cups fresh sliced strawberries
1/4 cup sugar
6 to 8 cooked crepes

1/2 cup heavy cream
2 tablespoons orange-flavored liqueur
1/2 pint vanilla ice cream, slightly softened

Sprinkle strawberries with sugar. Fill cooked crepes with strawberries. Whip cream until stiff. Gradually beat in liqueur, then ice cream. Spoon part of topping over strawberries. Fold crepes over. Spoon remaining topping over crepes. Makes 6 to 8 crepes.

Strawberries Savannah

Marinate the berries in orange juice or liqueur.

1 quart fresh strawberries (2 small boxes)
1/3 cup powdered sugar
1/3 cup orange juice *or* orange liqueur
1/2 cup heavy cream

1/2 cup dairy sour cream
1/4 teaspoon mace
2 tablespoons powdered sugar
12 to 14 cooked crepes

Mix strawberries, 1/3 cup powdered sugar, and orange juice or liqueur; refrigerate several hours. Combine heavy cream, sour cream, mace, and 2 tablespoons powdered sugar in small chilled bowl. Beat until it begins to thicken. Spoon strawberries and juice onto cooked crepes. Fold over. Top with whipped cream. Makes 12 to 14 crepes.

Orange Blossom Crepes

Cream cheese filling is simply delicious.

1 (3-oz.) pkg. cream cheese, softened
1 tablespoon milk
1/4 teaspoon almond extract
1/4 cup finely chopped toasted almonds
6 to 8 cooked crepes
1/4 cup butter
1/3 cup sugar
1 teaspoon lemon juice

2 teaspoons cornstarch
1/2 cup orange juice
1/4 cup orange liqueur
1 teaspoon grated orange peel
2 tablespoons cognac, warmed
2 tablespoons toasted sliced almonds
Orange sections (optional)

In small mixing bowl, mix cream cheese with milk, and almond extract. Add finely chopped almonds. Spread onto center of cooked crepes. Roll up and set aside. In large skillet or chafing dish, melt butter; stir in sugar and lemon juice. Dissolve cornstarch in orange juice. Add orange-juice mixture, orange liqueur, and grated peel to butter. Cook on low heat, stirring constantly, until thick and translucent. Put filled crepes in skillet or chafing dish of hot orange sauce; heat to boiling. Pour warm cognac over all. Ignite with long match. Spoon flaming sauce over crepes. Garnish with toasted sliced almonds and orange sections, if desired. Serve immediately. Makes 6 to 8 crepes.

Crepes Normandy

Apples and spice and everything nice!

1/4 cup butter or margarine
5 medium cooking apples, peeled and thinly
   sliced
1/4 cup brown sugar
1/2 teaspoon cinnamon
1 tablespoon brandy or cognac

1/4 cup orange juice
1 tablespoon grated orange peel
10 cooked crepes
2 tablespoons melted butter
Whipped cream or dairy sour cream

Heat butter in large skillet; add apples and sauté until translucent, stirring frequently. Add brown sugar and cinnamon; cook until sugar dissolves. Remove from heat. Add brandy, orange juice, and peel. Spoon about 2 tablespoons apple mixture on center of each cooked crepe. Fold over. Place in shallow baking pan. Brush with melted butter. Heat in 350°F (177°C) oven for 10 to 15 minutes. Serve with whipped cream or sour cream. Makes 10 crepes.

Orange Blossom Crepes

Crepes Helene

Impress unexpected guests with this quick and easy dessert.

12 cooked crepes
3/4 cup orange marmalade
1/4 cup finely chopped blanched almonds

2 tablespoons brown sugar
3/4 cup dairy sour cream
1 tablespoon grated orange peel

Spread each cooked crepe with about 1 tablespoon marmalade. Roll up and place in shallow baking pan. Combine almonds with brown sugar and sour cream. Spread over top of filled crepes. Sprinkle with orange peel. This may be done just before dinner and set aside until dessert time. Broil until bubbly. Makes 12 crepes.

Cinnamon Raisin Roll-ups

Use your left-over crepes for school-lunch goodies.

2 tablespoons butter
10 cooked crepes
1/4 cup sugar

1 1/4 teaspoons ground cinnamon
2/3 cup raisins

Spread thin layer of butter on each crepe; sprinkle with sugar, cinnamon, and raisins. Roll up; place in shallow baking pan. Bake at 350°F (177°C) for 5 to 8 minutes.

Brandied Mincemeat Crepes

Great holiday dessert—much easier to make than a pie.

1/3 cup brown sugar, packed
1 tablespoon cornstarch
3/4 cup water
2 tablespoons butter

2 tablespoons brandy
1 cup mincemeat, heated
8 warm cooked crepes

In small saucepan, combine sugar and cornstarch. Stir in water. Cook and stir until mixture boils and slightly thickens. Remove from heat. Stir in butter and brandy. Warm mincemeat. Fill cooked crepes with mincemeat; fold over. Spoon brandy sauce over. Makes 8 crepes.

Fruit Cake Crepes

Rich crepes filled with holiday goodies!

1/2 cup chopped candied fruits
1/2 cup raisins
1/2 cup chopped dates
1/2 cup walnuts, finely ground
1/3 cup milk

1/4 cup sugar
2 tablespoons butter or margarine
1/4 teaspoon almond extract
1 tablespoon rum
6 or 7 cooked crepes

Eggnog Sauce:
1 egg, slightly beaten
3/4 cup milk
2 tablespoons sugar

1 tablespoon brandy *or* 1/2 teaspoon vanilla
Nutmeg

In saucepan, combine candied fruits, raisins, dates, walnuts, milk, and sugar. Cook over low heat, stirring constantly, for 2 or 3 minutes or until mixture holds together. Remove from heat; add butter, almond extract, and rum. Spread on cooked crepes. Roll up loosely. Place in buttered baking pan. Heat in 350°F (177°C) oven for 10 to 15 minutes. Serve warm with eggnog sauce. Makes 6 or 7 crepes.

To make eggnog sauce:
In small, heavy saucepan, combine egg with milk and sugar. Cook over low heat, stirring constantly, until mixture coats spoon. Remove from heat; add brandy or vanilla. Serve warm or cool over warm Fruit Cake Crepes. Sprinkle with nutmeg.

Caramelized Orange Crepes

Caramelized sugar gives a different flavor to orange crepes.

1/3 cup sugar
1 cup orange juice
1 teaspoon grated orange peel
1 teaspoon lemon juice

3 tablespoons butter
2 tablespoons orange-flavored liqueur
10 to 12 cooked crepes

Put sugar in heavy skillet over moderate heat, shaking the pan occasionally until sugar melts and turns a light amber color. Remove from heat; add orange juice, grated peel, lemon juice, and butter. Return to heat and simmer 10 minutes, or until slightly thickened. Stir in liqueur. Dip crepes, one at a time, into hot orange sauce. Fold each crepe in half, then half again, forming a wedge shape. Serve hot. Makes 10 to 12 crepes.

To caramelize sugar, pour into small heavy skillet.

Heat over moderate heat, shaking the pan occasionally. Edges of sugar will melt and turn a caramel color.

Continue heating until all sugar melts and is a smooth caramel color.

Burgundy Fruit Crepes

A colorful fruit combination.

1/2 cup dry red wine
1/2 cup water
1/2 cup sugar
1 teaspoon pickling spices
1 tablespoon cornstarch
1 tablespoon water

1/2 cup sliced seeded grapes
1/2 cup orange segments, cut into bite-size
  pieces
1/2 cup pitted dates, chopped
8 to 10 cooked crepes
Whipped cream (optional)

In saucepan, combine wine, 1/2 cup water, sugar, and spices. Bring to a boil; simmer for 10 minutes. Dissolve cornstarch in 1 tablespoon water. Add to wine mixture; simmer several minutes or until thickened. Strain; cool. Pour over combination of grapes, oranges, and dates. Refrigerate several hours if possible. Fill crepes with fruits; fold over. Spoon any extra sauce over top. Garnish with whipped cream, if desired. Makes 8 to 10 crepes.

Sicilian Crepes

All the traditional Italian flavors!

1 lb. ricotta cheese
2 tablespoons light cream
1/3 cup sugar
2 tablespoons orange-flavored liqueur
1/3 cup chopped mixed candied fruit

1 (1-oz.) square semi-sweet chocolate, coarsely
  grated
12 to 15 cooked crepes
Powdered sugar

In medium bowl, beat cheese with cream. Add sugar and liqueur; beat until smooth. Stir in fruit and chocolate. Fill crepes; fold over. Refrigerate several hours. Dust with powdered sugar. Makes 12 to 15 crepes.

Dutch Fluff Crepes

Glamorize pie filling with fluffy sour cream topping.

1/2 cup dairy sour cream
2 tablespoons sugar
1/8 teaspoon almond extract
1/8 teaspoon ground mace

1/2 cup cottage cheese
10 cooked crepes
1 (21-oz.) can cherry *or* peach pie filling
1/4 cup slivered toasted almonds

Combine sour cream, sugar, almond extract, and mace in small mixing bowl. Refrigerate beaters and mixture in bowl until very cold. Beat until thick and almost double in volume. This takes about 5 minutes. Fold in cottage cheese; refrigerate until serving time. Fill cooked crepes with pie filling; fold over. Spoon sour cream sauce over crepes. Top with almonds. Makes 10 crepes.

French Cream Crepes with Raspberry Sauce

Make filling and sauce ahead and let crepes chill until dessert time.

3/4 cup sugar
1/2 cup flour
2 cups milk
4 eggs, beaten

2 tablespoons butter
1 teaspoon vanilla
11 or 12 cooked crepes

Sauce:
1 (10-oz.) pkg. frozen raspberries
1/4 cup sugar

2 tablespoons cornstarch

In saucepan, combine sugar and flour; stir in milk. Cook over low heat, stirring constantly, until thick. Remove from heat. Stir a small amount of hot mixture into beaten eggs, then return to the saucepan. Cook over low heat, stirring constantly, for about 2 minutes. Stir in butter and vanilla. Cool. Fill crepes; shape into a loose roll. Serve with raspberrry sauce. Makes 11 or 12 crepes.

To make sauce:
Thaw raspberries. In small saucepan, combine sugar and cornstarch. Stir in raspberries with juice. Cook over low heat, stirring until thick. Cool. Spoon over filled crepes just before serving.

Melba Peach Sundae Crepes

Really colorful and good!

1 (10-oz.) pkg. frozen raspberries
1/3 cup currant jelly
3 tablespoons butter
1/4 teaspoon almond extract

1 (1-lb.) can peach slices, drained
10 scoops vanilla ice cream
10 cooked crepes
1/4 cup slivered almonds

Thaw raspberries; force through a strainer. In saucepan, combine seedless raspberry purée, jelly, butter, and almond extract. Bring to a boil over moderate heat. Add peaches. Cool for several minutes. With large spoon, scoop ice cream onto each crepe; fold over. Spoon peaches and sauce over. Sprinkle with almonds. Serve immediately. Makes 10 crepes.

Black Forest Crepes

Ultimate elegance and taste!

2 (17-oz.) cans dark sweet pitted cherries
1 cup powdered sugar
2 tablespoons cornstarch
1/2 cup Italian almond-flavored liqueur

14 to 16 warm cooked crepes
1 cup dairy sour cream
1 (1-oz.) square semi-sweet chocolate, grated

Drain cherries, saving 1/3 cup juice. In saucepan, combine sugar and cornstarch; stir in liqueur and 1/3 cup cherry juice. Add drained cherries. Cook over moderate heat, stirring constantly until slightly thickened. Spoon cherries and sauce onto warm crepes; fold over. Spoon sour cream over top. Sprinkle with chocolate, serve immediately. Makes 14 to 16 crepes.

Melba Peach Sundae Crepes

Grasshopper Crepes

Really impressive and colorful filling for Chocolate Crepes.

2 cups miniature marshmallows or
   22 large marshmallows
1/3 cup milk
2 tablespoons white cream de cacao
3 tablespoons green creme de menthe
Green food color (optional)

1 cup heavy cream
12 cooked Chocolate Crepes *or*
   All-Purpose Crepes
Whipped cream (optional)
1/2 oz. semi-sweet chocolate

Heat marshmallows and milk in saucepan over low heat, stirring constantly, until marshmallows just melt. Refrigerate, stirring occasionally, until mixture mounds slightly when dropped from a spoon (about 1/2 hour). Stir creme de cacao, creme de menthe, and several drops green color into marshmallow mixture. Beat heavy cream until stiff. Fold green mixture into whipped cream. Fill cooked crepes; fold over. Chill until firm. Top with extra whipped cream, if desired. Grate chocolate or make chocolate curls; sprinkle over crepes. Makes 12 crepes.

In heavy, small saucepan, combine marshmallows with milk; heat until smooth.

Refrigerate melted marshmallow mixture until mixture mounds when dropped from a spoon.

Fold green mixture into whipped cream until well blended and smooth.

Lemon Dream Crepes

Better than lemon meringue pie!

1/2 cup butter (1 stick)	3 egg yolks, beaten
1 teaspoon grated lemon peel	3 whole eggs, beaten
1/2 cup lemon juice	1 cup heavy cream
1/8 teaspoon salt	18 to 20 cooked crepes
1 1/2 cups sugar	

In medium saucepan, melt butter; add lemon peel, lemon juice, salt, and sugar. Stir in beaten egg yolks and whole eggs. Cook over very low heat, beating constantly with a whisk, until mixture is shiny and thick. Cool. Whip cream. Fold one-half the whipped cream into lemon mixture and fill cooked crepes; fold over. Top with remaining whipped cream. Makes 18 to 20 crepes.

Lemon Soufflé Crepes

This filling is as light and delicate as a soufflé and must be served immediately.

2 tablespoons sweet butter	2 teaspoons grated lemon peel
3 tablespoons flour	2 egg whites
1/3 cup hot milk	2 teaspoons powdered sugar
2 egg yolks	16 to 18 cooked Dessert Crepes
2 tablespoons sugar	Sugar for top
2 tablespoons lemon juice	

In heavy saucepan, melt butter over low heat; stir in flour and cook 1 or 2 minutes. Remove from heat. Beat in hot milk. Return to heat; cook, stirring constantly, until mixture thickens. Immediately spoon into large bowl; beat in egg yolks, one at a time. Stir in 2 tablespoons sugar, lemon juice, and peel. In separate bowl, beat egg whites; gradually add powdered sugar and beat until stiff. Fold beaten whites into yolk mixture. Spoon about 1 heaping tablespoon of egg-lemon mixture on each cooked crepe. Carefully fold into quarters. Arrange in large shallow buttered baking pan. Lightly sprinkle sugar over top of crepes. Bake at 400°F (205°C) for 10 minutes. Serve immediately. Makes 16 to 18 crepes.

Butterscotch Meringue Crepes

Meringue topping adds glamor to butterscotch crepes.

1 (3 5/8-oz.) pkg. butterscotch pudding
2 cups milk
10 or 11 cooked crepes

3 egg whites
6 tablespoons sugar
1/4 cup chopped walnuts

In saucepan, combine pudding with milk. Cook over medium heat, stirring constantly until mixture comes to a full, bubbling boil. Cool about 10 minutes, stirring twice. Fill cooked crepes with puding mixture. Fold over; place in shallow baking pan. In small mixing bowl, beat egg whites until foamy. Gradually add sugar, beating until stiff peaks form. Spread meringue over tops of filled crepes. Sprinkle with nuts. Bake in 400°F (205°C) oven for 6 to 9 minutes or until meringue is light brown. Serve warm or cool. Makes 10 or 11 crepes.

Chocolate Eclair Crepes

Short-cut eclairs!

1 (3 1/4-oz.) pkg. vanilla pudding mix
1 1/2 cups milk
1 tablespoon rum *or* 1/2 teaspoon vanilla

1/2 cup heavy cream
10 to 12 cooked crepes

Glaze:
1 tablespoon butter or margarine
2 1/2 tablespoons sugar
1 (1-oz.) square unsweetened chocolate

2 tablespoons water
1/2 teaspoon vanilla

Prepare pudding mix according to package directions, *except* use 1 1/2 cups milk instead of the 2 cups called for. Bring to a boil; remove from heat and stir in rum or vanilla. Cover surface with waxed paper. Refrigerate until cool. Whip heavy cream until stiff. Fold into chilled pudding. Fill cooked crepes with pudding; fold over. Makes 10 to 12 crepes.

To make glaze:
In small saucepan, combine butter, sugar, chocolate, and water. Stir over low heat until chocolate melts and mixture is smooth. Add vanilla. Let stand about 5 minutes. Spoon over filled crepes. Refrigerate until serving time.

Strawberries & Cream Crepes

Everyone's favorite!

3 cups fresh strawberries
1/3 cup granulated sugar
1 cup cottage cheese

1 cup dairy sour cream
1/2 cup powdered sugar
10 to 12 cooked crepes

Slice strawberries; add granulated sugar and set aside. In blender, whip cottage cheese until smooth; stir in sour cream and powdered sugar. Fill crepes with about 2/3 of creamy mixture and berries; fold over. Top with remaining strawberries and cream. Makes 10 to 12 crepes.

Pear Crepes

For those who love ginger.

1 cup sugar
1/4 cup water
5 pears, peeled and thinly sliced

1/2 teaspoon vanilla
2 tablespoons finely chopped crystallized ginger
8 to 10 warm cooked crepes

Custard Sauce:
1/4 cup sugar
3 tablespoons flour
1 cup milk

1 egg, beaten
1/2 teaspoon vanilla

In skillet, combine sugar and water; cook over moderate heat for 5 minutes or until syrup is thickened. Add pears, vanilla, and ginger. Simmer until pears are tender. Fill crepes; fold over. Top with custard sauce. Makes 8 to 10 crepes.

Custard sauce:
Combine sugar and flour in saucepan. Stir in milk and cook over low heat, stirring constantly, until thickened. Remove from heat. Stir a little of the mixture into the beaten egg; return egg mixture to pan. Cook over low heat 2 or 3 minutes. Stir in vanilla. Makes about 1 1/4 cups custard.

Crepes Café Au Lait

Indescribably delicious!

10 cooked crepes
1/4 cup brown sugar, packed
1/8 teaspoon cinnamon

1/2 cup heavy cream
6 tablespoons coffee-flavored liqueur, heated
Whipped cream (optional)

Fold crepes in half, then half again; set aside. In skillet or chafing dish, combine brown sugar, cinnamon, and cream. Heat, stirring, but do not boil. Turn heat to low; add folded crepes. Turn each crepe to coat with sauce. Ignite liqueur. Pour flaming liqueur into skillet or chafing dish. Spoon flaming sauce over crepes. When flame dies, top with whipped cream, if desired, and serve. Makes 10 crepes.

Mocha Cheese Cups

Hot from the oven, these are quite puffy like a soufflé. They lose volume as they cool, but they are still delicious.

12 to 14 cooked crepes
2 eggs, separated
1/8 teaspoon salt
1/8 teaspoon cream of tartar
1/2 cup sugar
1 (8-oz.) pkg. cream cheese *and*
　1 (3-oz.) pkg. cream cheese

1/2 teaspoon instant coffee powder
1/2 square unsweetened chocolate, melted
2 tablespoons light rum
Powdered sugar

Line buttered muffin pans or custard cups with cooked crepes. Beat egg whites with salt and cream of tartar until peaks form. Gradually beat in *1/4 cup* sugar, beating until stiff but not dry. In another bowl, beat yolks, remaining *1/4 cup* sugar, cheese, and coffee powder until smooth. Add chocolate and rum to cheese mixture. Fold in beaten egg whites. Spoon into crepe-lined muffin pans or custard cups. Bake in 350°F (177°C) oven for 20 to 25 minutes. Cool 5 minutes before removing from pan. May be served warm or cool. Sprinkle with powdered sugar before serving. Makes 12 to 14 cups.

Jamocha Mousse

Rich and creamy!

1 (6-oz.) pkg. semi-sweet chocolate pieces
4 egg yolks
2 tablespoons rum
1 teaspoon instant coffee powder

4 egg whites
1/2 cup sugar
20 cooked crepes
Whipped cream (optional)

In saucepan, melt chocolate over very low heat. Add egg yolks, one at a time, beating after each addition. Remove from heat. Blend in rum and coffee powder. Beat egg whites until frothy; gradually add sugar, beating until stiff. Stir a small amount of beaten egg whites into chocolate mixture; then fold chocolate mixture into remaining egg whites. Fill cooked crepes; fold over and chill. Serve with whipped cream if desired. Makes 20 crepes.

Hungarian Chocolate Nut Crepes

Different, with a rich chocolate flavor!

Filling:
1 cup milk
1 1/2 cups ground walnuts
1/4 cup sugar

1/4 cup raisins
1 tablespoon grated orange peel
2 tablespoons rum

10 to 12 warm cooked crepes

Sauce:
4 (1-oz.) squares semi-sweet chocolate
2 tablespoons sugar
1 tablespoon cocoa
2 egg yolks

1 teaspoon flour
1/4 cup milk
1 tablespoon rum

Filling:

In saucepan, heat milk; mix in walnuts, sugar, raisins, and orange peel. Cook on very low heat, stirring constantly, for about 15 to 20 minutes. Add rum. Spread about 2 tablespoons filling on each crepe. Loosely roll up and keep warm.

Sauce:

Melt chocolate with sugar and cocoa over very low heat. Beat egg yolks, flour, and milk; add to chocolate. Heat, stirring constantly, but do not boil. Add rum. Pour over warm filled crepes immediately and serve. Makes 10 to 12 crepes.

Cherry Cream Stack

An extra special dessert! For a short-cut version, use canned cherry pie filling for the topping and packaged vanilla pudding between the layers.

Cream Filling:

1/2 cup sugar	2 cups milk
2 tablespoons flour	3 egg yolks, beaten
1 tablespoon cornstarch	1/4 teaspoon almond extract
1/4 teaspoon salt	

16 to 18 cooked crepes
Whipped cream (optional)

Cherry Topping:

1/2 cup sugar	1 teaspoon lemon juice
1 tablespoon cornstarch	2 tablespoons port wine
1 (16-oz.) can pitted red tart cherries	Several drops red food coloring
1/4 cup juice from cherries	

In saucepan, combine sugar, flour, cornstarch, and salt. Stir in milk. Cook, stirring constantly, until mixture thickens. Stir a little of the hot mixture into beaten egg yolks; then return egg mixture to pan. Cook over low heat, stirring, several minutes longer. Add almond extract. Cool. Spread cooled cream filling between crepes to make 2 stacks of 8 or 9 crepes each. Spoon cherry mixture over top of stacks. Garnish with whipped cream, if desired. Cut each stack into 6 or 8 pie-shaped wedges. Makes 12 to 16 servings.

Cherry Topping:

In small saucepan, combine sugar and cornstarch. Drain cherries, saving 1/4 cup juice. Stir drained cherries and 1/4 cup juice into sugar mixture. Cook, stirring constantly, over low heat, until thickened and translucent. Stir in lemon juice and wine. Cool to lukewarm. Spoon over top of stacks.

Sweet Chocolate Wedges

Prepare this rich, easy-to-make chocolate dessert ahead of time.

1 (4-oz.) pkg. sweet cooking chocolate	1 cup heavy cream, whipped
1 tablespoon water	10 cooked Dessert Crepes
2 egg yolks	Slivered almonds (optional)

Combine chocolate and water in saucepan over low heat; stir until chocolate melts. Add egg yolks, one at a time, beating well after each is added. Remove from heat; cool. Fold in whipped cream. Spread chocolate mixture over each crepe. Stack crepes on top of each other. Chill several hours. Cut into six wedges. Garnish with slivered almonds, if desired. Makes 6 servings.

Cherry Cream Stack

Chocolate Fondue

Really yummy!

6 (1-oz.) squares unsweetened chocolate
1 cup light cream
1 1/2 cups sugar
1/2 cup butter or margarine

1/8 teaspoon salt
3 tablespoons creme de cacao *or*
    coffee-flavored liqueur

In saucepan, melt chocolate in cream over very low heat. Stir in sugar, butter, and salt. Cook, stirring constantly, until smooth. Stir in liqueur. Pour into fondue pot; keep hot. Dip Fondue Dippin' Chips into sauce. Makes about 3 cups chocolate fondue.

Fondue Dippin' Chips

Ideal for a party! Prepare chips ahead of time and serve with dessert fondue. All-purpose crepes work fine, but dessert crepes are perfect.

6 cooked crepes
Powdered sugar

Cut each cooked crepe into quarters; then each quarter into 3 or 4 wedges, making 12 to 16 pieces from each crepe. Place on cookie sheet; bake in 400°F (205°C) oven for 6 to 8 minutes or until crisp and brown. Remove from oven. Sprinkle with powdered sugar. Use as dippin' chips for Chocolate Fondue. Makes 72 to 96 dippers.

Chocolate Peanut Pillows

For chocolate and peanut-butter fans!

1 (6-oz.) pkg. semi-sweet chocolate pieces
1/3 cup light corn syrup
1/4 cup light cream
1 tablespoon butter
1/4 teaspoon vanilla

1/4 cup peanut butter
10 small scoops chocolate or vanilla ice cream
10 cooked crepes
1/4 cup chopped peanuts

In saucepan, melt chocolate with corn syrup at low heat, stirring until blended. Stir in cream and heat to boiling. Remove from heat; mix in butter, vanilla, and peanut butter. Place small scoop of ice cream in center of each crepe. Fold sides of crepe over ice cream, then bottom and top. Press lightly to flatten and seal. Place folded edge down on dessert plate. Spoon sauce over and sprinkle with peanuts. Makes 10 crepe pillows.

Peanutty Chocolate Sundae

Make your own variation with your favorite ice cream.

1/2 cup chunky peanut butter
1/4 cup marshmallow creme
1/4 cup hot water
1/4 cup chocolate syrup

8 to 10 cooked crepes
Chocolate, chocolate chip, or vanilla ice cream
Marshmallow creme for garnish

In small skillet, combine peanut butter, marshmallow creme, hot water, and chocolate syrup. Heat and stir until well blended and warm. Fill crepes with ice cream. Fold over; top with warm sauce. Garnish with extra marshmallow creme. Serve immediately. Makes 8 to 10 crepes.

Flaming Berry Creams

Beautiful dark berry color with creamy center.

1/4 cup butter, softened
1 cup powdered sugar
2 tablespoons cassis liqueur
12 cooked crepes

1/4 cup raspberry *or* boysenberry jam
1/4 cup cassis liqueur, heated
Whipped cream (optional)

Beat butter and sugar until creamy; stir in 2 tablespoons liqueur. Spread butter mixture over each crepe. Spread about 1 teaspoon jam down the center of each. Roll up. Chill until ready to serve. Then heat in 400°F (205°C) oven for 8 to 10 minutes or until warm. Ignite 1/4 cup warm liqueur; pour over crepes. Spoon flaming liqueur over crepes. Serve warm, with whipped cream, if desired. Makes 12 crepes.

Spread butter mixture over each crepe, leaving a border of about 1/4-inch. Then spoon a strip of jam about an inch wide along the center of each.

Gently roll up crepe. Don't let mixture ooze out the ends. Then refrigerate to make filling firmer.

Fudge Sundae Crepes

If you're lucky enough to have fudge sauce left over, it keeps in the refrigerator for several days.

1/2 cup butter
1 cup sugar
1/8 teaspoon salt
1 teaspoon instant coffee powder
2 tablespoons rum
1/3 cup cocoa

1 cup heavy cream
1 teaspoon vanilla
15 to 18 cooked crepes
15 to 18 small scoops vanilla ice cream
Whipped cream (optional)

Melt butter in saucepan. Blend in sugar, salt, coffee powder, rum, and cocoa. Add cream. Simmer about 5 minutes, stirring occasionally. Remove from heat; add vanilla. Fill cooked crepes with ice cream. Spoon fudge sauce over filled crepes. Serve topped with whipped cream, if desired. Serve immediately. Makes 15 to 18 crepes.

Crepes A La Bananas Foster

Variation of Old New Orleans' favorite dessert.

4 bananas
1 tablespoon lemon juice
1/4 cup butter
1/2 cup brown sugar
1/8 teaspoon ground cinnamon

1/2 cup rum, warmed
8 cooked crepes
8 small scoops vanilla ice cream
1/4 cup chopped pecans

Peel and slice bananas. Pour lemon juice over bananas. Melt butter and sugar in skillet or chafing dish. Add bananas; sauté until just hot. Sprinkle with cinnamon. Remove pan from heat. Pour warmed rum over bananas; ignite with long match. Spoon sauce over bananas until flame burns out. Spoon bananas with sauce over crepes that have been filled with vanilla ice cream. Sprinkle pecans over crepes. Serve immediately. Makes 8 crepes.

Glazed Strawberry Crepes

Similar to the ever-popular glazed strawberry pie.

4 cups fresh strawberries (2 pint baskets)
1/2 cup water
2/3 cup sugar
2 tablespoons cornstarch

Several drops red food coloring
10 cooked crepes
1 cup whipped cream *or* scoops of vanilla
   ice cream

Wash and cap strawberries. Crush 1 cup of smaller berries. Slice large berries and set aside. In small saucepan cook 1 cup smaller berries with water until berries are soft. Sieve berries and return juice to pan. Combine sugar and cornstarch. Stir into strawberry juice. Cook over moderate heat, stirring constantly, until thickened. Add several drops of red coloring. Cool for about 5 minutes. Stir sliced berries into strawberry glaze. Fill crepes with strawberries and glaze. Fold over. Refrigerate for about 1/2 hour. Top each crepe with whipped cream or ice cream; serve immediately. Makes 10 crepes.

Blueberry Hill Crepes

Bananas are beautiful with the blueberries!

1 (10-oz.) pkg. frozen blueberries
1/2 cup sugar
1 tablespoon cornstarch
1/4 teaspoon nutmeg
1 tablespoon lemon juice

1 banana, sliced
Vanilla ice cream *or* orange sherbet
6 to 8 cooked crepes
Whipped cream (optional)

Thaw blueberries. In saucepan, combine sugar, cornstarch, and nutmeg. Stir in blueberries and lemon juice. Cook, stirring constantly, until thickened. Add sliced banana. Cool 5 to 10 minutes. Fill each crepe with scoops of ice cream. Fold over. Spoon warm sauce over filled crepes. Top with whipped cream if desired. Makes 6 to 8 crepes.

Tropical Medley

An easy-to-fix glamorous dessert! For a change, try lemon or pineapple sherbet instead of the ice cream.

1 banana
1 tablespoon lemon juice
1/2 cup apricot-pineapple preserves
1/4 cup rum

1/2 cup coconut
8 to 10 cooked Dessert Crepes
8 to 10 small scoops vanilla ice cream

Mash banana; stir in lemon juice. In small saucepan, combine mashed banana and lemon juice with preserves, rum, and coconut. Heat to boiling point. Spoon over crepes that have been filled with ice cream. Serve immediately. Makes 8 to 10 crepes.

Peanut Brittle Ice Cream Crepes

Crunchy peanut brittle topping is a pleasant surprise.

12 scoops vanilla ice cream
12 cooked crepes

1 cup heavy cream, whipped
1/2 cup crushed peanut brittle

Sauce:
1/4 cup butter or margarine
1 1/4 cups brown sugar
2 tablespoons light corn syrup

1/4 cup heavy cream
1 teaspoon vanilla

Scooping with a large spoon, fill crepes with ice cream; fold over. Top crepes with whipped cream, then crushed peanut brittle. Freeze. At serving time, spoon sauce over crepes and serve immediately. Makes 12 crepes.

Sauce:
Combine butter, sugar, corn syrup, and cream in small saucepan. Heat until butter melts; simmer mixture for 1 minute. Remove from heat; stir in vanilla. Cool about 5 minutes; serve over crepes.

Chocolate Almond Crunch

Like chocolate candy? You'll love these crepes!

Topping:

1/2 cup ground blanched almonds
1 tablespoon sugar

1 tablespoon melted butter

Filling:

1 1/2 cups miniature marshmallows or
   16 large marshmallows
1/2 cup milk

1 (8-oz.) milk chocolate candy bar
1 cup heavy cream

12 to 14 cooked Chocolate Crepes *or* All-Purpose Crepes

Topping:

Combine ground almonds with sugar and butter. Spread on cookie sheet. Heat in 400°F (205°C) oven for 6 to 8 minutes or until light brown. Cool.

Filling:

In saucepan heat marshmallows, milk, and chocolate over low heat, stirring constantly until mixture is smooth. Refrigerate until mixture mounds slightly when dropped from a spoon (about 30 to 45 minutes). Beat cream until stiff. Fold chocolate mixture into whipped cream. Fill cooked crepes; fold over. Sprinkle with cool almond topping. Makes 12 to 14 crepes.

Make topping ahead of time so it can cool. Grind almonds in food chopper or blender. Spread ground almonds mixed with sugar and melted butter on cookie sheet to heat.

Cool chocolate mixture before folding into whipped cream.

Fill cooked crepes with finished chocolate mixture; fold over. Then spoon cooled crunchy topping over all.

Quickie Caramelized Cream Crepes

A short-cut dessert you can make very quickly.

8 cooked crepes
1 (16-oz.) can peach *or* apple pie filling

1 cup dairy sour cream
1/3 cup brown sugar

Fill crepes with pie filling. Fold over. Place on broiler pan. Spread sour cream over top of each filled crepe. Sift brown sugar evenly over sour cream. Broil until sugar begins to caramelize. Makes 8 crepes.

Waikiki Crepes

Flavors from the tropics with a yogurt tang.

1 (8-oz.) can crushed pineapple, well drained
1 (11-oz.) can mandarin oranges, drained
1/2 cup flaked coconut
1 (8-oz.) carton orange or pineapple yogurt

1/3 cup sliced maraschino cherries
8 to 10 cooked crepes
Powdered sugar

Combine pineapple, oranges, and coconut with yogurt. Stir in cherries, saving a few slices for top. Fill crepes with fruit mixture. Sprinkle with powdered sugar; top with extra cherry slices. Makes 8 to 10 crepes.

Chocolate Torte

A many-splendored chocolate stack.

1 (6-oz.) pkg. semi-sweet chocolate pieces
1/2 cup butter or margarine
1/4 cup water
4 slightly beaten egg yolks
2 tablespoons powdered sugar

1 teaspoon vanilla
7 or 8 cooked crepes
1/4 cup whipped cream or topping
1/4 cup toasted sliced almonds, cooled

In small saucepan, heat and stir chocolate, butter, and water until well blended; cool slightly. Stir in eggs, sugar, and vanilla. Chill until it has spreading consistency (about 1 hour). Spread crepes with mixture; stack. Spread whipped cream over top layer; sprinkle with almonds. Cut into 6 or 8 wedges.

Crepe Igloos

A spectacular surprise—with ice cream in the middle.

8 to 10 scoops chocolate ice cream
8 to 10 cooked crepes
4 egg whites

1/2 teaspoon cream of tartar
1/2 cup sugar

Scoop ice cream with a large spoon. Place one scoop in center of each crepe. Fold over sides of crepe, then bottom and top, forming a pocket. Place in shallow baking pan and freeze until firm. If possible, keep filled crepes in freezer in the baking pan overnight or at least 3 to 4 hours, or until you are ready to spread them with meringue. It is necessary to *work quickly* so the ice cream remains firm and the pan cold. The result is dramatic!

Just before serving, beat eggs and cream of tartar until soft peaks form. Gradually add sugar, beating until stiff. Working quickly, spread meringue over frozen filled crepes in baking pan, making sure all edges are sealed. Bake in extremely hot oven—500°F (260°C)—until meringue is brown or about 3 minutes. Serve immediately. Makes 8 to 10 crepes.

SAUCES

A sauce can "make" or "break" a crepe. If the sauce is compatible with the other ingredients in the crepe, everyone thinks the crepe is excellent. If the flavor of the sauce clashes with the meat, fish or vegetable in the crepe, the crepe is a disaster rather than a creation.

Throughout the book I have given the recipe with appropriate sauce on the same page so you won't have to look in several sections to make one recipe. Those sauces are not repeated in this section, but you may want to use them with other recipes for your own concocting. This section is designed as an added convenience for your own creations. Perhaps you can use sauces with foods you have on hand—or with some of your traditional family combinations.

Some of these sauces are very elementary and basic. I included them for those who may not remember the basic proportions. Starting with *White Sauce,* for example, you can vary it by adding cheese, bouillon, herbs, eggs or olives. When properly seasoned and mixed with a bit of meat or poultry, the basic sauce transforms crepes into elegant main dishes.

Although several of the other sauces are fairly simple, they are designed to help you out when you are in a jam. Like when your husband unexpectedly brings the boss home for dinner, or the day before payday when you're trying to make some leftover chicken feed the whole family. Most of these helpful sauces are made from ingredients you have on hand. They require little preparation and cooking time.

In grocery shopping, you may have found a bargain on some variety or cut of meat that I have not included in the book. I hope these sauces will help stretch your budget and enable you to present impressive meals to your family and friends.

Don't overlook the dessert sauces for last-minute or make-ahead desserts. All of them can be made with very little time and effort. They transform plain vanilla ice cream into a thing of beauty and a joy to eat. If hungry teenagers are part of your family, you know how they devour sweet desserts. The *Hot Mocha Fudge Sauce* and *Peanut Butterscotch Sauce* will be sure winners with them.

If you can keep these dessert sauces on hand long enough to be concerned about storage, you can store them in a covered container in the refrigerator several days. In fact you might like to make up a double batch and keep them on hand for a midnight snack or an extra-special dessert.

Hot Mocha Fudge Sauce

Keep this rich fudge sauce on hand for spur-of-the-moment dessert crepes.

1 (14-oz.) can sweetened condensed milk
2 (1-oz.) squares unsweetened chocolate
1/3 cup water

2 teaspoons instant coffee powder
2 tablespoons orange liqueur

In top of double boiler, heat milk, chocolate, water, and coffee powder over simmering water, stirring constantly, until mixture thickens—about 20 minutes. Remove from heat; stir in liqueur. Serve warm. May be kept in refrigerator several weeks and heated when needed. Spoon over crepes filled with custard, ice cream, or whipped cream. Makes about 1 3/4 cups sauce or enough for 12 to 15 crepes.

Peanut Butterscotch Sauce

Rich and peanutty!

1/2 cup undiluted evaporated milk
1 (6-oz.) pkg. butterscotch bits
1/2 cup miniature marshmallows

1/4 cup peanut butter
1/4 cup chopped peanuts
1 teaspoon vanilla

Heat milk, butterscotch bits, and marshmallows over low heat, stirring constantly, until mixture is smooth. Stir in peanut butter and peanuts; blend until smooth. Remove from heat; add vanilla. Makes about 1 1/2 cups sauce.

Especially good over ice cream filled crepes

Apricot Sauce

A dessert sauce to improve all kinds of fruit.

1 1/2 tablespoons cornstarch
2 tablespoons sugar
1/8 teaspoon salt
1 cup apricot nectar

1/2 cup light corn syrup
1 tablespoon butter
1/4 teaspoon almond extract

In small saucepan, combine cornstarch with sugar and salt. Stir in apricot nectar and corn syrup. Cook over medium heat, stirring constantly, until thickened. Remove from heat. Add butter and almond extract. Cool. Makes about 1 1/2 cups sauce.

Serve over cooked crepes filled with banana or coconut ice cream, pineapple sherbet, or fresh mixed fruit.

Praline Sauce

A hint of maple flavor makes this pecan sauce delightful.

1/4 cup butter or margarine
1/2 cup powdered sugar
2 tablespoons maple syrup

1/4 cup water
1/2 cup finely chopped pecans

In saucepan, heat butter until light brown. Cool slightly. Gradually mix in sugar. Stir in syrup and water. Bring to boil; simmer 1 minute. Add nuts. Serve warm. Makes 1 cup sauce.

Try over apple, peach, or pear-filled crepes.

Pineapple Coconut Topping

Excellent on crepes filled with butter-pecan or vanilla ice cream.

1/3 cup butter or margarine
1 cup packed brown sugar
1/4 cup milk

1 (8-oz.) can crushed pineapple, well drained
1/2 cup flaked coconut

In small saucepan, combine butter and brown sugar; stir over low heat until butter is melted. Add milk. Bring to boil; simmer 3 minutes. Remove from heat. Stir in pineapple and coconut. Makes 1 1/2 cups sauce.

White Sauce

A basic sauce used in many crepe fillings. Add other seasonings for variations; combine with cooked chicken, fish, meat, or vegetables.

2 tablespoons butter or margarine
2 tablespoons flour

1/4 teaspoon salt
1 cup milk

Melt butter in saucepan over low heat. Blend in flour and salt. Add milk; cook over moderate heat, stirring constantly, until mixture thickens. Add spices or herbs, as desired. Makes about 1 cup.

Avocado Sauce

Great for crepes with Mexican-type fillings.

1 avocado, peeled and mashed
1/2 cup dairy sour cream
2 teaspoons lemon juice

1/2 teaspoon grated onion
1/4 teaspoon salt
1/4 teaspoon chili powder

Using fork or spoon, combine avocado with remaining ingredients. Serve as sauce or topping for enchiladas, tacos, or burritos made with crepes.

Creole Sauce

A bright sauce to pep up your crepes!

2 tablespoons butter or margarine
1/2 cup chopped onion
1/4 cup chopped green pepper
1/4 cup chopped celery
1 medium tomato, peeled and chopped

1 (8-oz.) can tomato sauce
1 (3-oz.) can sliced mushrooms, drained
1/4 teaspoon salt
1/8 teaspoon garlic salt

In saucepan, melt butter. Add onion, green pepper, celery, and tomato. Cover and simmer until vegetables are tender. Stir in remaining ingredients. Cook another 2 or 3 minutes. Makes about 2 cups.

Try this sauce over crepes filled with seafood or eggs.

Remoulade Sauce

A traditional sauce for shrimp, but can be used over other seafoods.

1 cup mayonnaise
1/2 cup dairy sour cream
2 teaspoons Dijon mustard
1 tablespoon chopped capers
1 tablespoon chopped sweet pickle

2 teaspoons chopped parsley
1/4 teaspoon dried basil leaves, crumbled
1/8 teaspoon dried tarragon leaves, crumbled
1 tablespoon lemon juice

Combine ingredients; chill until serving time. Makes 1 2/3 cups sauce.

Bordelaise Sauce

Perks up beef crepes!

3 tablespoons butter or margarine
3 tablespoons flour
1 cup beef bouillon
2 tablespoons red wine
1 teaspoon instant minced onion

1 tablespoon lemon juice
1/2 teaspoon dried tarragon, crushed
1 teaspoon chopped parsley
1/8 teaspoon brown bouquet sauce for gravy

In small saucepan, melt butter. Stir in flour, then bouillon and wine. Cook over low heat, stirring constantly, until thickened. Add onion, lemon juice, tarragon, parsley, and bouquet sauce. Bring to a boil. Makes about 1 1/4 cups sauce.

Serve with meat-filled crepes.

Lemon Butter

Especially good on fish.

1/4 cup butter or margarine
1 tablespoon lemon juice
1/4 teaspoon salt

Dash cayenne pepper
1 tablespoon finely chopped parsley

Melt butter; stir in remaining ingredients. Brush or spoon over fish, seafood, broccoli, or asparagus crepes.

Herb Butter

Perks up beef or vegetable crepes.

1/2 cup soft butter or margarine
1 tablespoon chopped parsley
2 teaspoons chopped chives

1/8 teaspoon dry mustard
1/8 teaspoon onion salt
1/8 teaspoon crushed thyme

Beat butter until fluffy. Stir in remaining ingredients. Serve over warm crepes filled with meats or vegetables. Makes 1/2 cup herb butter.

Wine Cheese Sauce

A rich sauce you'll like on meat or vegetables.

1/2 cup butter
1/3 cup flour
1/2 teaspoon salt
2 cups milk

1/4 cup dry sherry
1/2 teaspoon dill weed
1 (3-oz.) pkg. cream cheese, softened and cubed

Melt butter; stir in flour, then salt and milk. Cook, stirring until sauce thickens. Add sherry, dill, and cream cheese. Stir over low heat until smooth. Makes about 3 cups sauce.

Serve warm over crepes filled with roast beef, broccoli, or asparagus.

Sour Cream Sauce

Complements beef crepes.

2 tablespoons flour
2 tablespoons melted butter or margarine
3/4 cup milk
1 teaspoon horseradish

1/4 teaspoon salt
1/8 teaspoon pepper
1/2 teaspoon Worcestershire sauce
1/2 cup dairy sour cream

In small pan, stir flour into butter. Add milk, then seasonings. Cook, stirring constantly, on low heat until slightly thickened. Remove from heat; stir in sour cream. Serve over beef or vegetable crepes. Make 1 1/8 cups sauce.

Low-Calorie Sour Cream

Here's a way to cut down calories.

1/4 cup non-fat milk (liquid)
1 tablespoon lemon juice

1 cup cottage cheese

Combine milk, lemon juice, and cottage cheese in blender jar. Blend until smooth. Use as filling or topping for blintzes, or with vegetable crepes. If used on a dessert crepe, add a bit of vanilla or almond flavoring.

INDEX

SPICE CHART

NAME AND DESCRIPTION	COMPATIBLE WITH:
Allspice Color—brown Flavor—spicy, sweet, mild, pleasant	All cranberry dishes, spice cakes, beef stew, baked ham, mincemeat and pumpkin pie, tapioca & chocolate pudding
Anise Color—brown with tan stripes Flavor—sweet licorice aroma and taste	Coffee cake, rolls, cookies, all fruit pie fillings, sweet pickles, stewed fruits
Basil Color—light green Flavor—mild, sweet	All tomato dishes, green vegetables, stews, shrimp and lobster dishes
Bay Leaves Color—light green Flavor—very mild, sweet	Vegetables, stews, shrimp, lobster, chicken dishes, pot roasts
Caraway Color—dark brown with light brown stripes Flavor—like rye bread	Cheese spreads, breads and rolls, cookies, vegetables, roast pork
Cardamom Color—cream-colored pod, dark brown seeds Flavor—bitter-sweet	Danish pastry, coffee cake, custards, sweet potato and pumpkin dishes
Cayenne Color—burnt orange Flavor—hot	Deviled eggs, fish dishes, cooked green vegetables, cheese souffles, pork chops, veal stew
Celery Seed Color—shades of brownish green Flavor—bitter celery	Meat loaf, fish chowders, cole slaw, stewed tomatoes, rolls, salad dressings
Chili Powder Color—light to dark red Flavor—distinctive, hot	Mexican cookery, chili, beef, pork and veal dishes, Spanish rice
Cinnamon Color—light brown Flavor—sweet and spicy	Coffee cakes, spice cake, cookies, puddings, fruit pies, spiced beverages, sweet potato and pumpkin dishes
Cloves Color—dark brown Flavor—spicy, sweet, pungent	Ham, apple, mince & pumpkin pies, baked beans, hot tea, spice cake, puddings, cream of pea and tomato soups
Cumin Color—gold with a hint of green Flavor—salty sweet	Deviled eggs, chili, rice, fish
Curry Powder Color—Predominantly rich gold Flavor—exotic with heat	Eggs, fish, poultry, creamed vegetables, chowders, tomato soup, salted nuts
Dill Color—greenish brown Flavor—similar to caraway, but milder and sweeter	Pickling, potato salad, soups, vegetables, salad dressing, drawn butter for shellfish
Ginger Color—tan Flavor—spicy	Cookies, spice cake, pumpkin pie, puddings, applesauce, stews, French dressing

NAME AND DESCRIPTION	COMPATIBLE WITH:
Mace Color—burnt orange Flavor—similar to nutmeg, exotic	Fish, stews, pickling, gingerbread, cakes. Welsh rarebit, chocolate dishes, fruit pies
Marjoram Color—green Flavor—delicate	Lamb chops, roast beef, poultry, omelets, stews, stuffings
Mint Color—green Flavor—sweet	Jelly, fruit salad, lamb and veal roast, tea
Mustard Color—light to dark brown Flavor—spicy, sharp	Pickling, Chinese hot sauce, cheese sauce, vegetables, molasses cookies
Nutmeg Color—copper Flavor—exotic, sweet	Doughnuts, eggnog, custards, spice cake, coffee cake, pumpkin pie, sweet potatoes
Oregano Color—green Flavor—strong	Pizza, spaghetti sauce, meat sauces, soups, vegetables
Paprika Color—red Flavor—very mild	Poultry, goulash, vegetables, canapes, chowders
Parsley Color—green Flavor—mild	Soups, salads, meat stews, all vegetables, potatoes
Pepper Color—black or white Flavor—spicy, enduring aftertaste	Almost all foods except those with sweet flavors. Use white pepper when black specks are not desired.
Poppy Seeds Color—blue-gray Flavor—crunchy, nutlike	Breads and rolls, salad dressings, green peas
Rosemary Color—green Flavor—delicate, sweetish	Lamb, beef, pork, poultry, soups, cheese sauces, potatoes
Saffron Color—red-orange Flavor—exotic	Rice, breads, fish stew, chicken soup, cakes
Savory Color—green Flavor—mild, pleasant	Scrambled eggs, poultry stuffing, hamburgers, fish, tossed salad
Sesame Seeds Color—cream Flavor—crunchy, nutlike	Breads and rolls, cookies, salad dressings, fish, asparagus
Tarragon Color—green Flavor—fresh, pleasant	Marinades of meat, poultry, omelets, fish, soups, vegetables
Thyme Color—olive green Flavor—pleasantly penetrating	Tomato dishes, fish chowder, all meats, potatoes
Turmeric Color—orange Flavor—mild, slightly bitter	Pickles, salad dressings, seafood, rice